READING GAMES FOR MIDDLE AND UPPER GRADES

By
Flora C. Fowler

East Tennessee State University

MSS EDUCATIONAL PUBLISHING COMPANY, INC.
655 Madison Ave., New York, N. Y. 10021

Library of Congress Cataloging in Publication Data

Fowler, Flora C
  Reading games for middle and upper grades.

    1. Reading games. 2. Reading (Secondary education)
I. Title.
LB1632.F68   1974   428'.4'07   74-8367
ISBN 0-8422-5182-0
ISBN 0-8422-0429-6 (pbk.)

ABOUT THIS BOOK

Reading Games for Middle and Upper Grades is a collection of activities which may be used with students to aid in building various reading skills and to help promote positive attitudes toward reading.

Each activity in this book has been field-tested with students of various levels. As a result the following suggestions are made:

1. Although these exercises are designed for the intermediate grades, individual questions within exercises may range in difficulty from primary grade level to senior high level. Teachers using these activities should select those questions which they deem appropriate for the maturity level of their students and should formulate additional questions on the same level.

2. Some activities provide examples of how to build comprehension skills, some provide examples of how to build word recognition skills, and some provide both. However, do not limit the skill development to those skills for which examples are provided in this book. Also, do not hesitate to use an activity to build both skill areas during the same or different sessions.

3. After becoming familiar with an activity through the questions provided and perhaps through questions which the teacher has constructed, the students themselves should be encouraged to write questions. Learning and interest can be greatly enhanced through such attempts.

4. Many activities are designed for participation by only a few students at a time. When this occurs, the class should be divided into as many teams as there are participants. Therefore, members of the audience are "rooting" for their team member rather than viewing the activity passively. Also, after answering a specific number of questions or after the passage of a predetermined amount of time, students representing teams may be changed--thus involving a larger number of students in this activity.

5. Many activities are based on the procedures used in a television program. If possible, students should view the program before playing the game. All rules, however, are not identical to those on the television version but have been adapted for classroom use.

6. If the first attempt to use an activity seems unsuccessful, do not give up. In many cases students are just becoming familiar with the activity during the first exposure. Try it again.

7. Before interest wanes, participation in the activity should cease. Students should stop an activity while they still have the desire for further participation in that activity. By doing so, they will not tire of it as easily and will want to participate again on future occasions.

No part of this book may be duplicated without written permission of the author.

ABOUT THE MATERIALS BOOK

This book was written to be used with an accompanying <u>Materials Book for Reading Games for Middle and Upper Grades</u> (hereafter referred to as <u>Materials Book</u>), which is a collection of stories, answer sheets, exercise sheets, forms for teacher and student use, transparency originals, etc., which are needed in order to play these games. These materials were included in a separate book in order to be printed on 8½" x 11" perforated pages for the users' convenience.

An explanation of each item which is included in the <u>Materials Book</u> is provided at the end of each exercise appearing in this book. Explanations are not repeated in the <u>Materials Book</u>.

All of the materials in the <u>Materials Book</u> may be duplicated, may be projected through an overhead or opaque projector, or may be used as the teacher desires in order for the students to participate in the activities. No part of the book may be duplicated for any other reason without written permission of the author.

CONTENTS

THE WHO WHAT OR WHERE READING GAME

ACTIVITY NO. 1

THE WHO, WHAT, OR WHERE READING GAME

Purpose

The purpose of **THE WHO, WHAT, OR WHERE READING GAME** is to promote interest and enthusiasm in the development of students' necessary reading and reading-related skills through a competitive and challenging activity. Through this version of this activity, each member may participate with each student competing against himself.

Skills

The specific skills of comprehension, word recognition, and vocabulary development may be developed through this activity. A basic knowledge of addition, subtraction, and multiplication will be needed to compute individual scores.

Materials Needed

1. The chalkboard may be used on which to write the category and the odds for each "W", _or_ a board may be made from a sheet of poster paper (22" x 28") with slots for categories and odds. Several removable tabs for categories (4" x 10") and six removable tabs for odds (3" x 6½") will be needed for this board. A sample board, reduced in size, is shown at the end of this explanation.

2. A transparency may be used instead of poster board. A form for a transparency is found in the _Materials Book_. The categories and odds may be written in with a grease pencil.

3. One individual student response blank will be needed for each student participating. A sample blank form is provided.

4. (Optional) Forms for the preparation of Who, What, and Where questions and answers may be used. These forms aid in organization when the students are preparing the exercise. They may also be filed for future use. A blank form is provided following this explanation and in the _Materials Book_ for duplication if desired.

Preparation and Instructional Procedures

1. A selected story should be read by the students.

2. Several categories should be selected on which a <u>Who</u> question, a <u>What</u> question, and a <u>Where</u> question are written. Categories may pertain either to the skills being measured or to the content of the story. See Appendix for examples of categories.

3. Odds must be chosen for each question, depending on its level of difficulty. "E" (for Even) is assigned to relatively easy questions. The numbers "2", "3", or "4" would be assigned to more difficult questions. The higher the odds, the more difficult the question.

8

4. Each student is given a "Student Individual Response Blank" on which to write his responses.

5. The first category and odds are revealed. The student (by category number 1) "locks in his wager" by circling a Who, What, or Where, and an amount. After these two items have been circled by each student, all wagers have been locked in and the questions may be asked.

6. The "Who" question may be asked first. Each student who circled the "Who" answers that question by writing in the space provided for the answer.

7. The answer is revealed. The student checks his answer by circling the check or X.

8. For those who responded correctly, their circled amount is multiplied by the "Odd", (E=1). This amount is written in the column "Amount for each question". This amount is then added to $125 (in last column) for the first question or to the previously accumulated totals for following questions.

9. For those who responded incorrectly, DO NOT MULTIPLY THEIR WAGER BY THE ODDS! Simply subtract the amount circled from $125 for the first question or from their previously accumulated totals for following questions.

10. The "What" and "Where" questions proceed the same way.

11. One to ten questions may be handled in the above fashion. The last question is called the "Final Question" and the response is made on the bottom line of the response blank. For this question, the student locks in his "W" in the same manner as before, but he is free to wager any part or all of his accumulated money. He does this by writing in the desired amount by the words "Unlimited Wager". Repeat steps for asking and answering questions. Final scores are then determined and the winner is declared.

Origin of the Activity

THE WHO, WHAT, OR WHERE READING GAME was based on the currently popular television program "The Who, What, or Where Game." Procedures for this activity were adapted from this television program for educational use in the reading classroom.

Items Provided

The following items are provided in this book and/or in the accompanying Materials Book:

1. Page 9 in this book shows a sample Who, What, or Where board made of poster paper.

2. Page 10 in this book and page 3 in the <u>Materials Book</u> provide an "Individual Student Response Blank" for this game. This may be duplicated for each participant.

3. Page 11 in this book and page 4 in the <u>Materials Book</u> provide a form which may be duplicated to use for preparing questions for this game.

4. Pages 12-15 in this book and pages 5-12 in the <u>Materials Book</u> contain a sample story which may be duplicated for use with this game.

5. Pages 16-17 in this book provide questions from the sample story for use with this game.

6. Page 13 in the <u>Materials Book</u> contains a blank form which may be used instead of a poster board or chalkboard to play this game. In the rectangle near the middle, write in with a grease pencil the category; in the three small rectangles near the bottom, write in the odds. These may be erased with paper towels at the end of each round.

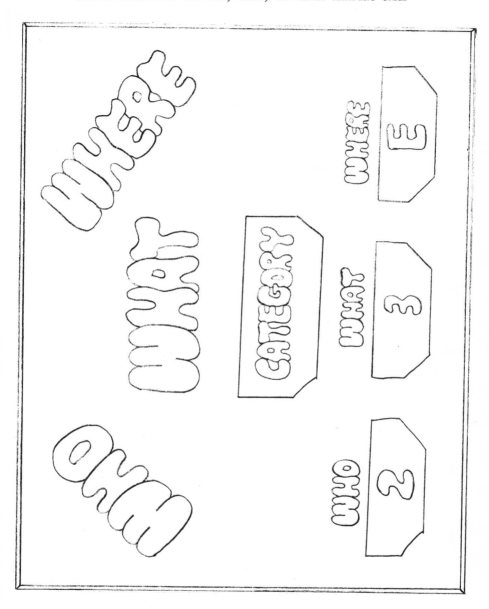

INDIVIDUAL STUDENT RESPONSE BLANK FOR THE WHO, WHAT OR WHERE READING GAME

NAME _____

Category Number	W: (Circle One)	Amount: (Circle One)	Answer		Amount for Each Question	Accumulated Total $125
1	Who What Where	$0-5-10-15-20-25-30-35-40-45-50		✓ X		
2	Who What Where	$0-5-10-15-20-25-30-35-40-45-50		✓ X		
3	Who What Where	$0-5-10-15-20-25-30-35-40-45-50		✓ X		
4	Who What Where	$0-5-10-15-20-25-30-35-40-45-50		✓ X		
5	Who What Where	$0-5-10-15-20-25-30-35-40-45-50		✓ X		
6	Who What Where	$0-5-10-15-20-25-30-35-40-45-50		✓ X		
7	Who What Where	$0-5-10-15-20-25-30-35-40-45-50		✓ X		
8	Who What Where	$0-5-10-15-20-25-30-35-40-45-50		✓ X		
9	Who What Where	$0-5-10-15-20-25-30-35-40-45-50		✓ X		
10	Who What Where	$0-5-10-15-20-25-30-35-40-45-50		✓ X		
Final Question	Who What Where	Unlimited Wager: $		✓ X		
					GRAND TOTAL	

FORM FOR PREPARING QUESTIONS FOR THE WHO, WHAT, OR WHERE READING GAME

Reading Selection: _____

Category: _____

"W"	Odds	Question	Answer
Who			
What			
Where			

Category: _____

"W"	Odds	Question	Answer
Who			
What			
Where			

Category: _____

"W"	Odds	Question	Answer
Who			
What			
Where			

A GHOST STORY

by Douglas Norman

The old Bennett house had stood empty and forsaken for years in the little town of Cornersville. At one time it had been a stately mansion, alive with happy parties, echoing with the laughter of many guests. But that had been long ago. Now no one would go near the house. It was, according to local legend, haunted.

No one really knew how the story got started. It was talked that the youngest daughter of the very rich family living in the mansion had had an unhappy love affair. She was said to have fallen in love with a man her father considered far beneath the social status of their family, and he forbade his daughter to marry the handsome young man.

"If I cannot marry my beloved, I will die, and this house will forever be cursed," she said. After that, she never left the house and never came out of her room when her father would have parties to try to help her meet young, rich men. Gradually, the parties grew fewer, and the house became quieter. The daughter stayed mostly in her room, or walked the halls of the great house at night, crying out the name of her loved one. She became ill and took to her bed. One night, exactly 12 months after her father had sent her lover away forever, the beautiful young daughter died.

Heartsick over what he had done, the father closed the mansion and left the little town, never to return. Afterwards, several families lived in the house, but none for long. Strange, supernatural things happened to the house and those who attempted to occupy it. At night, weird cries and moans could be heard, and sometimes a ghostly apparition could be seen walking the halls. Several of the people who lived in the house went insane, and the mansion came to have such a bad reputation that no one would move there, no matter how desperate they might be for shelter. Several drifters, unaware of this fact, broke into the house to find a place to sleep out of the weather, but were never seen again. At night, if one listened closely, he could hear moans and cries coming from the house-- sounds which no human could make.

Or so went local legend.

Not far from the deserted mansion stood the town's blacksmith shop. This was at the turn of the century, and horses, wagons and buggies had not been replaced by the automobile. The blacksmith was an important man in this era. He was depended on to keep vehicles in good condition for both business and pleasure purposes, much as do today's mechanics.

Tom Chestnut was the blacksmith, and he was known as one of the strongest, bravest men in the region, as well as one of the most handsome. Tom was able to handle the meanest animals brought to his shop, and when there was an occasional flare-up of trouble in town, Tom could be depended on to quiet the ruckus if the sheriff could not get there from the county-seat 10 miles away. Tom was strong enough to bend horseshoes with his bare hands. His body was muscular, his features well formed, and his good looks were enhanced by his coal-black hair.

Or so went local legend.

Tom also had a keen sense of humor. He had bought a book from a mail order catalog, and by slowly reading the book, Tom had learned how to throw his voice. (Tom had gotten as far as the fourth grade in school and was considered one of the better educated persons of his community, even though he did rough work with his hands.)

Sometimes Tom would make it seem that his voice was coming from the glowing coals of the forge in his blacksmith shop, and unsuspecting visitors would almost jump out of their bib overalls. Then Tom would laugh and laugh, and his cronies who were in on the gag would laugh too.

One day, Tom pulled his joke on a man who did not think it was very funny to be frightened by a "voice" coming from red-hot coals. Instead of joining in the laughter from Tom's cronies, as victims usually did once they recovered from their fright, the man grew sullen.

"You think you're so big and brave that you don't mind scaring people," he snarled at Tom. "Why don't you see just how brave you are? Why don't you spend a night at the old Bennett house? I've heard that no one has done it and lived. Why don't you do it? Then we'll see just how brave you are."

Tom's cronies got the man calmed down, and he soon went on his way. But the talk around the blacksmith shop drifted back to the Bennett house. It was as if someone had brought up a subject that people had been avoiding, and had reminded Tom and his friends of the morbid fascination which the old house held for them.

"Tom," said one of his cronies, "why don't you do it?"

"Do what?" muttered Tom, pretending he didn't know what the man was talking about.

"Why don't you spend a night at the old Bennett house? Why don't you just show folks that you aren't scared to stay a night there?"

"I'm not scared of anything," Tom replied, his face reddening. If there was one thing Tom didn't like, it was someone even hinting that he was afraid. Yet, deep down, Tom had a dread of the old Bennett house. He avoided walking past it at night when he could, and he thought he had heard strange noises coming from the house, especially on nights when the clouds hung low and lightning flashed and thunder rolled across the sky. In fact, this was about the only kind of night on which Tom would walk past the old mansion. The road by the old house was a short-cut to his home, and when rain threatened, Tom sometimes would hurry past the darkened mansion. When the weather was better, Tom found it more convenient to take a longer way home.

Deep down Tom knew something which no one else knew. He was afraid. He was really frightened, filled with the kind of dread that makes a man's back ache and his hands become cold, by only one thing. That was the Bennett house.

He could never explain it to himself, and he did not try very often. Yet, in the dark corners of his mind, Tom sensed that the old, empty mansion held evil for him, that it was perhaps the one thing he couldn't overcome with strength and bravery.

"Well, if you aren't scared of anything," said another crony as Tom pounded on a horseshoe, "why don't you do it?"

"Who wants to spend a night in a dusty old house?" Tom asked. "It's a crazy thing to do. When a man could be home in his own bed, why stay a whole night in a place like the old Bennett house? Why, everybody around here would think I was touched in the head."

"I do believe," said one crony, turning to another and sensing a chance to needle Tom, "that he's afraid to do it. Old Tom is making excuses. We've found the one thing that Tom's afraid of. Wait 'til I tell the folks down at the general store."

"Hold on," Tom said, his voice rising. "I said I wasn't afraid, and I'm not. I just think it's silly to waste time like that."

"Well, just so it won't be a complete waste of time," said one of his friends in the tone of voice the villagers used when they talked of trading horses or knives, "I'll bet that each one of us would be willing to put in a quarter, and give all the money to you after you had stayed the night at the Bennett house."

Now 25 cents was not a small sum of money at this time in our history, and soon Tom's friends had collected almost 10 dollars from people around the community. Tom knew with a sickening sense of fear that he could not now back down. He must go through with it, or the whole town would know of his secret. They would know that Tom Chestnut, the bravest and strongest man in town, was afraid of an old, empty house.

A date was set, and as the time drew near when Tom would spend his night in the Bennett place, his sense of dread grew. He tried to convince himself that he was being silly, that there was no such thing as ghosts, and besides, he could take on anything and anybody, in this world or any other.

Near twilight on the appointed day, a large crowd had gathered close enough to the old Bennett house to see it, but far enough away that they could scatter at the first sign of any supernatural goings-on. They cheered when Tom, carrying his bedroll and a kerosene lantern, walked down the road toward them.

"Here he comes."

"We knew you weren't afraid."

"We'll be waiting for you in the morning."

Now Tom's agreement was that he would stay in the house from nightfall to dawn. His cronies were to meet him when he emerged the next morning and give him the $10 purse which had been collected.

As Tom opened the gate of the wooden fence surrounding the old house, the sky suddenly darkened. A black cloud was moving in from the west, moving fast, and even now a lacework of lightning could be seen around its edges. As Tom walked down the path from the gate to the front door, the first dull boom of thunder could be heard.

The crowd looked at the sky, and at the old mansion which suddenly had taken on an even more ominous appearance than usual, and the people slowly began backing away.

"Good luck, Tom!" shouted one of his friends as Tom put his hand on the doorknob of the entrance to the mansion. "It looks like rain, so we won't linger. But we know you're a man of your word. We know you'll keep your part of the bargain without us here to check up on you."

Tom pushed open the door and vanished inside the house. Suddenly there was a loud thunderclap. Huge drops of rain began to fall. The spectators, who had been walking faster and faster, suddenly broke and ran.

All during that night, there was one of the worst storms ever witnessed by even the oldest residents of the little town. There was almost a continuous roar of thunder, and lightning streaked across the sky, flashing so brightly that it lit up the town as if by day. Those brave enough to peer from behind their closed shutters could see the old Bennett house, since it sat on a little hill at the edge of town. They were sure that Tom Chestnut, the bravest and strongest man in town, was all right, but deep down they experienced a strange sense of dread.

It was still raining, although not as hard, the next day as dawn drew near. Only a small number of persons, mostly Tom's cronies, gathered near the old mansion. They huddled close together, talking in hushed voices. As the sky lightened in the east, they edged somewhat nearer the old Bennett house. They could not see the sun, for low clouds still scudded across the sky. The wind rose, fell, and rose again.

"Tom," shouted one of his buddies. "Are you in there? You can come on out now and collect your bet. You've been there long enough. You can come out now, Tom."

Suddenly the wind died, and the rain seemed almost to stop. The group heard the creaking of rusty hinges, and slowly the front door of the old Bennett house opened. A figure appeared.

The crowd gasped. Even in the low light of dawn, they could see it was Tom. But he had changed. His hands shook, and he almost fell as he stumbled down the front steps. He walked with a peculiar shuffle, dragging one leg behind him. His eyes stared wildly. His hair, which had been coal-black the day before, had turned solid white. He could not speak, only make strange, unintelligible sounds. He somehow seemed much smaller and older than the day before.

Tom never recovered. He lived out his life unable to communicate with those around him, seemingly unable even to see them through eyes that constantly reflected horror and terror.

The old Bennett mansion burned soon thereafter. There was much talk among the townspeople that someone had put a torch to it. The more skeptical ones scoffed, saying that the old timbers of the house were so dry that the mansion was a tinderbox, ready to burn at the first spark, and that it was struck by lightning during a windstorm.

But it was a fact that the house was completely destroyed during a storm when lightning flashed, thunder roared, and the winds howled. It was a storm much like that which occurred when Tom Chestnut spent the night in the mansion.

As the house burned, some onlookers swore that they heard a crescendo of moans and screams coming from the flames. Others said it was only the wind and fire blowing through the rooms of the old structure. Some said that the house had to be destroyed by fire to rid it of the ghosts within it. The scoffers insisted that the only ghosts which exist are in the minds of men.

What do you think?

SAMPLE QUESTIONS FOR THE WHO, WHAT, OR WHERE READING GAME

Story: "A Ghost Story"

Category: The Bennetts

"W"	Odds	Question	Answer
Who	E	Who in the Bennett family had an unhappy love affair?	The daughter
What	E	What did the father do to the daughter to make her so unhappy?	He forbade her to marry the man she loved.
Where	3	Where was the Bennett house located? (In what city?)	In Cornersville

Category: Reading

"W"	Odds	Question	Answer
Who	E	Who had ordered a book to read?	Tom
What	2	What had Tom learned to do by reading about it in this book?	To throw his voice
Where	3	From where had Tom ordered his book?	From a mail order catalog

Category: Tom Chestnut - Before

"W"	Odds	Question	Answer
Who	E	Who chided Tom into spending the night in the Bennett house?	His cronies (or friends)
What	2	What was Tom's occupation?	He was a blacksmith
Where	E	Where did Tom walk when the weather was bad when he was on his way home?	By the old Bennett house

18

Category: __Tom Chestnut - After__

"W"	Odds	Question	Answer
Who	E	Who was Tom able to communicate with now?	No one
What	E	What was the color of Tom's hair now?	White
Where	2	Where did Tom almost fall as he was coming out of the Bennett House?	On the front steps

Category: __Objects__

"W"	Odds	Question	Answer
Who	E	Who could bend horseshoes with his bare hands?	Tom Chestnut
What	3	What two objects did Tom take in the house with him?	A bedroll and a kerosene lantern
Where	2	From where would Tom sometimes make people think his voice was coming?	From the glowing coals

FINAL QUESTION

Category: __Words__

"W"	Odds	Question	Answer
Who	3	Who are scoffers?	People who make fun of something
What	4	The sky had taken on an even more ominous appearance than usual. What does the word ominous mean?	Foreshowing evil
Where	E	Where did several drifters spend the night in this story?	In the Bennett House

19

SPIN THE BOTTLE

Purpose

The purpose of SPIN THE BOTTLE is to capitalize on an activity which the students already find highly reinforcing in order to develop a greater interest in one which they currently might enjoy less.

Skills

General reading and reading-related skills may be developed through this activity. (A basic knowledge of addition and subtraction will be needed to compute individual scores.)

Materials Needed

One individual SPIN THE BOTTLE Board and answer sheet will be needed by each student participating in this activity. A sample board is shown on the cover of this explanation and a blank form and answer sheet are provided in the **Materials Book.**

Preparation and Instructional Procedures

1. A selected story should be read by the participating students. This activity may be used independently of specific reading selections. An example might be centering the questions around isolated word recognition skills. See samples following this explanation.

2. Several questions should be prepared based on the content of this story. These questions should have answers of "True", "False" or "Insufficient Information."

3. Each student is given a SPIN THE BOTTLE Board and an Answer Sheet.

4. **Before** each question is read to the class, each student spins the bottle on his board.

5. Each student then records the number spun in the appropriate column on his answer sheet.

6. The question is then read to the class.

7. All students respond by circling the words "True", "False", or "Other" (meaning not enough information was provided to answer True or False) on their answer sheet.

8. Decisions of correctness of responses are made and recorded.

9. For correct responses, the number spun is added to the beginning score of 2,000 which is shown on the answer sheets. Each following correct response is added to the accumulated total.

21

10. For incorrect responses, the number spun is subtracted from the total. (Students _may_ have minus totals; however, since everyone starts with 2,000, minus totals are unlikely.)

11. At the end of the game the students with the highest accumulated totals are declared the winners.

Items Provided

The following items are provided in this book and/or in the accompanying Materials Book:

1. Page 21 in this book and page 14 in the Materials Book show a student response sheet. One sheet will be needed by each student each time the game is played.

2. Page 22 in this book contains examples of questions which may be used without a specific reading selection. These are used to build various word recognition skills. Use them as a guide to construct others for the needs of your class.

3. Page 15 in the Materials Book may be duplicated and used as the cover of the SPIN THE BOTTLE boards. For preparation, do the following:

   a. Make one copy of this sheet for each student you have in your class

   b. Adhere this sheet to heavy construction paper or to poster board.

   c. From poster board, cut out one bottle for each board you are making.

   d. Using a paper hole punch, punch a hole in the middle of this bottle

   e. Fasten bottle in the middle of the board with paper fasteners. These boards are now ready to use.

SPIN THE BOTTLE
Student Answer Sheet

Question Number	Number Spun	Answer					Total 2,000
1		True	False	Other	Right	Wrong	
2		True	False	Other	Right	Wrong	
3		True	False	Other	Right	Wrong	
4		True	False	Other	Right	Wrong	
5		True	False	Other	Right	Wrong	
6		True	False	Other	Right	Wrong	
7		True	False	Other	Right	Wrong	
8		True	False	Other	Right	Wrong	
9		True	False	Other	Right	Wrong	
10		True	False	Other	Right	Wrong	
11		True	False	Other	Right	Wrong	
12		True	False	Other	Right	Wrong	
13		True	False	Other	Right	Wrong	
14		True	False	Other	Right	Wrong	
15		True	False	Other	Right	Wrong	
16		True	False	Other	Right	Wrong	
17		True	False	Other	Right	Wrong	
18		True	False	Other	Right	Wrong	
19		True	False	Other	Right	Wrong	
20		True	False	Other	Right	Wrong	
					GRAND TOTAL		

(For use without a specific reading selection)

1.	The word <u>knowledge</u> has three syllables.	False
2.	<u>Small</u> is an antonym for <u>tiny</u>.	False
3.	<u>B-l-u-e</u> and <u>b-l-e-w</u> are homonyms.	True
4.	The words <u>met</u> and <u>bed</u> have the same vowel sounds.	True
5.	The word <u>dishonestly</u> has five syllables.	False
6.	The fifth letter of the word <u>position</u> is <u>i</u>.	False
7.	The words <u>gnaw</u> and <u>know</u> have the same first letter.	False
8.	The words <u>rodeo</u> and <u>embarrass</u> have the same number of syllables.	True
9.	The words spelled <u>s-n-o-w</u> and <u>p-l-o-w</u> rhyme with each other.	False
10.	The words <u>point</u> and <u>boy</u> have the same vowel sounds.	True
11.	The root or base words of <u>exportation</u> and <u>transport</u> are the same.	True
12.	The words <u>leave</u> and <u>return</u> are synonyms.	False
13.	The words <u>t-h-r-o-u-g-h</u> and <u>c-o-u-g-h</u> have the same final sound.	False
14.	The third letters of the words <u>scramble</u> and <u>street</u> are the same.	True
15.	The word <u>knight</u> has four different sounds.	False
16.	The last letter of the words <u>picnic</u> and <u>hike</u> are the same.	False
17.	The words <u>t-h-o-u-g-h</u> and <u>b-l-o-w</u> rhyme with each other.	True
18.	The words <u>store</u> and <u>fist</u> contain the same consonant blend.	True
19.	The words <u>t-h-i-n</u> and <u>t-h-e-n</u> have the same initial sound.	False
20.	The suffixes in the words <u>promotion</u> and <u>produce</u> are the same.	False
21.	The <u>ch</u> in the words <u>a-c-h-e</u> and <u>c-h-i-n</u> have the same sound.	False
22.	The words <u>fish</u> and <u>hat</u> have at least one identical sound.	False

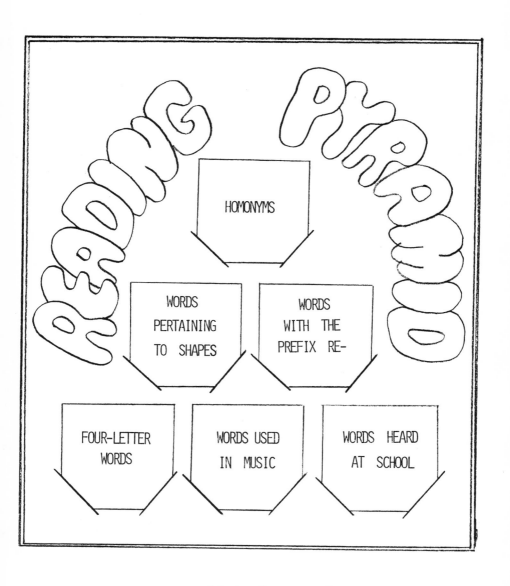

READING PYRAMID

HOMONYMS

WORDS PERTAINING TO SHAPES

WORDS WITH THE PREFIX RE-

FOUR-LETTER WORDS

WORDS USED IN MUSIC

WORDS HEARD AT SCHOOL

ACTIVITY NO. 3

READING PYRAMID

Purpose

The purpose of READING PYRAMID is to promote interest and enthusiasm in the development of the students' necessary reading and reading-related skills through a thought-provoking and competitive activity.

Skills

The primary skill to be enhanced in READING PYRAMID is that of vocabulary development. Other skills such as phonics or general reading skills may also be developed.

Materials Needed

1. Some means of conveying the categories will be needed. This may be done in one of two ways:

   a. An overhead or opaque projector may be used to reveal all categories for phase one of the game by using the materials found in the **Materials Book**.

   b. A READING PYRAMID board may be made from a sheet of poster paper. It would look similar to the one on the cover of this explanation. If this board is used, several category cards which would fit into the spaces on the pyramid will be needed. These cards may be made from construction or poster paper or may be large index cards.

2. Small number cards may be used to indicate the number of correct responses for each team. This same information, however, may be written on the chalkboard.

3. Some means of revealing the items to the person giving the clues will be necessary. If there is no audience desiring to see the items as the game is played, items may be written on a small index card and handed to the player, or the sheets in the **Materials Book** may be given to the player. If there are those desiring to watch, a transparency may be prepared so all may view. If a transparency is used, items are uncovered one at a time as they are either guessed or skipped.

4. A stopwatch or clock with a second hand is needed.

Preparation and Instructional Procedures

1. The class is divided into two teams. Two members from each team may participate at a time. Rotation of participating members should occur as teacher or students desire. In this manner all students are either participating or are "rooting" for their team members.

PHASE I:

2. The READING PYRAMID board or transparency is prepared to reveal six categories from materials which the students have encountered in their reading. These six categories may all be seen at once, and their place on the pyramid has no significance as to point value or difficulty.

3. For each of these six categories, approximately 10 items under each category should be prepared in advance. (Examples of categories and items are in the Materials Book.) The items may be revealed to the player in one of two ways:

   a. The 10 items may be written on small index cards and handed to each player as his turn comes to give clues for the items. In this manner, however, no one but the person holding the card can see the clues.

   b. If it is desired that an audience see the items as the clues are given, items should be flashed on a screen via an overhead or opaque projector.

4. The players on the first team together select a category from anywhere on the board and decide who will give the clues and who will receive them. The one giving the clues sits facing the screen if a transparency is used. The other team member sits with his back to the screen or in a position where he cannot see the card with the written items. When time is called, member with items begins giving clues for each item as rapidly as possible. These clues may be synonyms, descriptions, examples, blanks in sentences, or any verbal response to cause his partner to say the correct item. He may give any clue in order to elicit the correct word or phrase from his partner. However, he must take caution not to say all or part of any word used as an item. If he does this, the narrator says, "Inappropriate clue" and players must go on to the next item. The reasons for having to skip it may be explained after the time limit is over in order not to consume part of the allotted time. Players should be encouraged to talk as rapidly as possible giving either word, phrase, or sentence clues. Items are taken one at a time in the order as they appear. If a transparency is used, items are revealed one at a time and clues are guessed or skipped. It should be explained in advance that difficult items may be skipped if the player giving the clues is unfamiliar with the items or if the team member does not seem to know the correct response. Items may be returned to if time permits.

5. Sixty seconds (or any other desired previously determined period of time) are allowed for each of these categories. (It is best to have a person selected to be responsible only for keeping time.)

6. Score is kept by accumulating the number of correctly guessed items in each round.

7. Teams alternate selecting categories and guessing items until all six categories have been used. Members on each team rotate the giving and receiving of clues.

8. After all six categories have been used, the team with the highest number of points gets a chance to go to the final READING PYRAMID board, or to phase 2.

PHASE II:

9. These two players on the winning team now view the final READING PYRAMID board. The player who decides to give clues sits facing the board or screen and his partner sits out of its view.

10. This final READING PYRAMID board contains six hidden categories. In this final round, significance is placed on the location of the category in the pyramid. Players must begin with the bottom left square, proceed to bottom middle, bottom right, middle left, middle right, then to the top. Points are awarded according to the **following** **$50 for each on bottom row, $100 for middle, and $200 for top.** (NOTE: The television version of this game awards $10,000 if all categories are guessed within the allotted time period. The awarding of extra points in the classroom version is optional.)

11. The interaction of this phase, however, is quite different from that of phase 1. One category at a time is revealed to the team member viewing the board. <u>He must give as clues only examples of items</u> <u>which would fit into that category; and his team member attempts</u> <u>to guess what the category is.</u> Any other clue will cause the item to be discarded and no points will be awarded for that item. For example, with a category of "States," the player may say, "Tennessee, Virginia, Maryland, etc." to cause his partner to say "States," but he may <u>not</u> give a clue such as "a territory," "a unit of a nation," or other definitive material.

12. As a category is revealed, players either give a correct response, give misclues (same rules apply as in phase 1), or skip the item. Each following category is uncovered and attempted until all have been tried. Items may be returned to if time remains.

13. A time period of two minutes (or other previously determined period of time) is allowed.

14. The round is over upon completion of the final READING PYRAMID. Several rounds may be played in one class period. The team with the highest accumulated number of points at the end is declared the winning team.

Origin of Activity

READING PYRAMID was based on the currently popular television program, "$10,000 Pyramid." Procedures for this activity were adapted from this television program for educational use in the reading classroom.

Items Provided

The following items are provided in this book and/or in the accompanying Materials Book:

1. The bottom of this page and pages 28-30 in this book provide the teacher with a copy of the warm-up item, and three complete rounds of the activity.

2. Pages 16-42 in the Materials Book contain transparency originals in large type of these same items for use with an overhead projector. These pages may be extracted from the book and used with blank transparency film to make transparencies without additional typing or preparation.

SAMPLE ITEMS FOR READING PYRAMID

WARM-UP ROUNDS

These items may be used to familiarize the students with the procedures of READING PYRAMID. For these items, have all students in the classroom participating at once in pairs--one facing the screen and one looking in the opposite direction. Reveal all items at once and let them proceed at their individual rates. After each round, discuss possible clues and misclues. Check for any misunderstandings in the game.

Words Beginning with sl-

Sleep	Slaw	Slope
Sly	Slide	Slick
Slim	Slap	
Slow	Sleigh	

Titles of Magazines

Seventeen	Woman's Day	Family Circle
Life	Playboy	McCalls
Look	Boy's Life	
Reader's Digest	Redbook	

FINAL WARM-UP ROUND

50	-	Foreign Languages	100	-	Words Used in Science
50	-	Words Beginning with pr-	100	-	Words Ending in -ly
50	-	Round Things	100	-	Words on Menus

After students have understood the procedures through these warm-up rounds, divide the entire class into two teams. Two from each team may participate at a time, and participating members may change for each category, if desired.

Each category on this page is typed IN LARGE TYPE

on a separate page in the Materials Book for use with an overhead or opaque

projector.

SAMPLE ITEMS FOR READING PYRAMID

READING: VOCABULARY DEVELOPMENT

Four-letter Words
Girl	Lion	Cars
Hand	Desk	Knee
Sink	Frog	
Book	Beef	

Words Used in Music
Piano	Sharp	Drums
Songs	Organ	Flat
Records	Soprano	
Bass	Sing	

Words Pertaining to Shapes
Triangle	Cube	Cone
Square	Octagon	Hexagon
Circle	Diamond	
Rectangle	Pentagon	

Words Heard at School
Principal	Gradecard	Teacher
Library	Fail	Office
Student	Bus	
Textbook	Cafeteria	

Homonyms
Red - Read	Blue - Blew	Board - Bored
No - Know	Not - Knot	Cent - Scent - Sent
Right - Write	Rode - Road	
Meet - Meat	Mail - Male	

Words with the Prefix Re-
Rerun	Reply	Resign
Retire	Report	Respond
Repeat	Request	
Reduce	Repair	

FINAL READING PYRAMID
50 - Words Used in Mathematics	100 - Plurals of Words
50 - Words That are Opposites	100 - Words Found on Road Signs
50 - Two-letter Words	200 - Words Heard in Television Commercials

Each category on this page is typed IN LARGE TYPE on a separate page in the Materials Book for use with an overhead or opaque projector.

READING: PHONICS

Words with /oi/ sound

Point	Roy	Annoy
Joy	Oil	Employ
Moist	Boy	
Toys	Avoid	

Words Ending with -sh

Fish	Dish	Sash
Wash	Flesh	Hush
Brush	Wish	
Flash	Mash	

Words Rhyming with All

Fall	Call	Haul
Tall	Wall	Install
Ball	Mall	
Paul	Gall	

Words with Long e Sound

Sleep	Me	We
Heat	Tree	Tea
Dream	Meat	
Flea	The	

Words Beginning with Str-

Street	Stream	Straw
Strong	Stretch	Strip
Straight	Strike	
Strange	String	

One Syllable Words

Dog	Pen	Plate
Car	Watch	Leg
Hat	Spoon	
Nail	Ear	

FINAL READING PYRAMID

50 - Words Containing Long o Sound	100 - Pairs of Rhyming Words
50 - Words Beginning with Br-	100 - Words Containing -th-
50 - Words Ending with -ch	100 - Two Syllable Words

Each category on this page is typed I N   L A R G E   T Y P E

on a separate page in the Materials Book for use with an overhead

or opaque projector.

SAMPLE ITEMS FOR READING PYRAMID

READING: GENERAL

Types of Written Materials

Books

Stories

Songs

Poems

Plays

Letters

Newspaper Articles

Essays

Reports

Magazine Articles

Famous Characters in Books

Lassie

Hardy Boys

Raggedy Ann

Nancy Drew

Snow White

Heidi

Bambi

Tom Thumb

Pecos Bill

Robinson Crusoe

Types of Books

Catalogs

Dictionary

Encyclopedia

Notebook

Textbook

Workbook

Braille Books

Telephone Books

Almanac

Atlas

Comic Strip Characters

Dagwood

Nancy

Charlie Brown

Li'l Abner

Donald Duck

Phantom

Born Loser

Andy Capp

Campus Professor

Priscilla

Parts of a Book

Index

Tables of Contents

Chapters

Pages

Cover

Title Page

Glossary

Contents

Preface

Bibliography

Things We Read

Books

Newspapers

Road Signs

Maps

Magazines

Billboards

Labels

Telephone Books

Menus

Mail

FINAL READING PYRAMID

50 - Fairy Tales

50 - Book Titles

50 - Characters in Mother
         Goose Rhymes

100 - Authors

100 - Parts of a Newspaper

200 - Short Stories

Each category on this page is typed I N   L A R G E   T Y P E

on a separate page in the Materials Book for use with an overhead

or opaque projector.

SIR CARDS

ACTIVITY NO. 4

SIR CARDS

Purpose

The purpose of exercises using SIR (Student Individual Response) CARDS is to allow each individual student to respond to every question asked by the teacher in a question-answer period. In a class of 30 students this one-to-one response rate is compared to one out of 30 chances for each student to respond to a question asked by the teacher. In addition, the teacher can know within seconds which students have not responded correctly to each question. The SIR CARDS may be used primarily with many other games and activities included in this program, but may also effectively be used independently.

Skills

Both word recognition and comprehension skills may be developed through the use of SIR CARDS. Oral responses, however, are limited.

Materials Needed

The only materials needed for this exercise are a red, green, and a yellow SIR Card for each student. Cards are 2" x 3" with 1" x 1½" color shapes pasted on the card's surface. Library card pockets to store the three cards for each student are optional.

Preparation and Instructional Procedures

1. If word recognition skills are to be developed through this activity, they may be developed either with or without the reading of a specific selection. If comprehension skills are to be developed, a selected story should be read by the students.

2. Students must understand the use of the SIR CARDS, as follows:

   When the teacher asks a question to the class, no oral responses are given. Each student, instead, responds by holding up one of the three colored cards which have been given to him. Each color denotes a specific response previously agreed upon by the class. The following might be typical:

	For True-False Questions	For Multiple-Choice Questions	For Number Responses
Green	True Yes	(a)	1 One
Red	False No	(b)	2 Two
Yellow	Insufficient Information to Respond	(c)	3 Three

These colors may correspond to those of traffic lights: Green means true, or everything is all right to go ahead; red means stop, there's something wrong; and yellow means to take caution.

3. Teacher must prepare questions with answers which may be indicated through the use of the SIR Cards.

4. The teacher proceeds with this exercise by allowing the students to respond to the prepared reading questions by holding up one of the cards after each question. Discussion should follow if some students do **not** respond correctly. After all students understand the answer, the teacher should proceed to the next question. An optional procedure might call for scores to be kept for each initial correct response and for high scorers to be recognized.

Adaptations of Exercise

Any color, number, word, or symbol coded cards may be used as adaptations of this explanation. Also, other colors may be added to indicate additional responses. Many of the exercises and activities included in this book may include the use of the SIR Cards as an adaptation of the original activity.

Suggested Teaching Sequence

It is suggested that the teacher begin with simple exercises designed to familiarize the students with the use of the SIR Cards. The teacher may then proceed by (a) allowing the students to construct exercises for the use of these cards following the reading of a selection, or (b) using the cards in conjunction with other exercises as explained in their adaptations.

READING
JOKER'S WILD

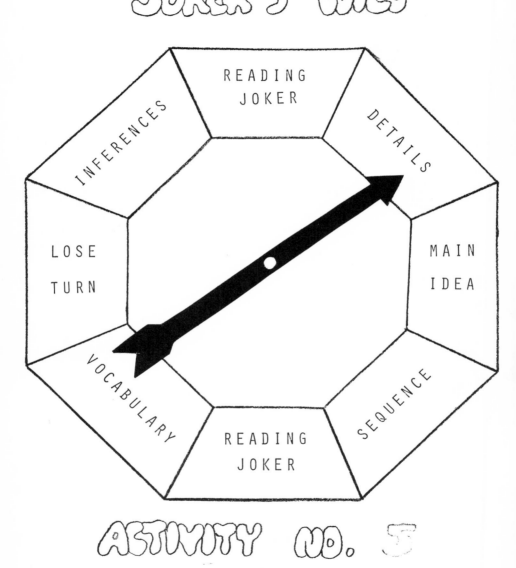

ACTIVITY NO. 5

Purpose

The purpose of READING JOKER'S WILD is to promote interest and enthusiasm in the development of the students' necessary reading and reading-related skills through a thought-provoking and competitive activity.

Skills

The specific subskills of comprehension may be developed through this activity.

Materials Needed

1. Three READING JOKER'S WILD boards will be needed for this activity. A sample board is shown on the cover of this explanation. It is possible to suffice with just one board which may be twirled three times.

2. Several category cards to be attached to the board will be needed if it is desired that the categories be changed. The board on the cover is designed to be a permanent board to build those specific comprehension skills.

3. A transparency may be used instead of poster board. A form for this transparency is in the Materials Book.

4. (Optional) Play money may be used to identify the amount accumulated by each individual. This same information may be written on the chalkboard.

Preparation and Instructional Procedures

1. Information on which questions are based should be decided by the teacher and students. This may be from the following sources:

    a. Any reading selection which the students have read or will read may be used. Questions based on this selection will be the subskills of reading comprehension. (See examples of these types of questions following this explanation.)

    b. Questions may be based on the word recognition skills with which the students have been involved.

    c. Questions may be based on vocabulary terms which students have encountered.

    d. Questions may be based on general knowledge of the language arts areas.

2. After selecting the categories, prepare approximately five questions for each one. (Number of questions prepared will depend upon the needs of the participating group.)

3. Divide class into two or three teams. One member from each team will participate at a time. Rotation of members will occur as the teacher or students desire. In this manner, all students are either directly participating or "rooting" for their team member.

4. Allow the participating members to face the boards or transparency. Allow the one on the first team to twirl three times.

5. The possibilities are as follows:

Outcome of three spins	Player's choice	Possibl Value
All three different	Select one	$50
One pair	Select the pair	$100
One pair	Select one other than pair	$50
Joker and two different	Select joker and one	$100
Joker and pair	Select joker and pair	$200
Two jokers	Select joker and remaining	$200
Three jokers	Select joker and category	$300
Lose turn and any combination	Player loses turn	$0

6. After twirling and selecting a category, if necessary, the player is asked a question from that category. If answer is correct, player gets the amount in "Possible Value" column above.

7. The opposing team member(s) take their turn and the game continues until a predetermined amount of money has been earned (such as $500) or until the class time has elapsed.

Origin of Activity

READING JOKER'S WILD was based on the currently popular television program "Joker's Wild". Procedures for this activity were adapted from this television program for educational use in the reading classroom.

Items Provided

The following items are provided in this book and/or in the accompanying Materials Book:

1. Pages 37-38 in this book and pages 43-45 in the Materials Book contain a sample story to be used to illustrate READING JOKER'S WILD.

2. Pages 39-41 in this book contain questions which have been prepared for the selected story for use with READING JOKER'S WILD.

3. Page 46 in the Materials Book contains a form which may be used to make a transparency for READING JOKER'S WILD. From poster paper cut out an arrow similar to the one on the cover of this exercise. Use a paper fastener to attach this to the transparency. For reinforcement cut out of manilla folders two circles about the size of a fifty-cent piece and paste on the front and back of the transparency where the paper fastener will go through. These may also be used to hide the ends of the paper fastener.

VIEW FROM A FLY'S EYE

by Larry Crosswhite

        Most people probably think that we flies lead pretty dull lives.
Well, this couldn't be farther from the truth for this fly. I just got
back from my annual trip to the beach, and believe me I experienced what
no human will ever come close to. Let me tell you about it. It was the
third day of my vacation, (yes flies take vacations too) and this was one
I'll never forget. I had decided to tour the coastal areas of North
Carolina and South Carolina and was just outside of Willmington, N. C.,
when hunger overtook me. It was well past 1:00 and I hadn't eaten since
early morning. My first response was to head straight toward the nearest
hamburger stand. This time of the day is a literal picnic for us flies at
such places. But then I remembered that this was to be an experience with
nature. I had promised myself to live off the land. So, not listening
to what my stomach was telling me, I took off for the nearest swamp. I was
flying along really getting into this nature bit, when all of a sudden I
was hit by an indescribable aroma. Circling around, nearly frantic with
hunger, I spotted the most beautiful hunk of what looked like fresh ground
hamburger lying there among the swamp grass just waiting for me to feast.
That was about all the invitation that was necessary at the moment. I
immediately made a beeline (excuse the pun) for this inviting meal.
Executing a nearly perfect landing, I was about to dig in, when all of a
sudden, darkness surrounded me. "What's this," I thought, "an eclipse?
A sudden storm?" Then it dawned on me what had happened. I had become
the gullible victim of a Venus Fly Trap. I had heard stories here and there
about terrifying "fly-eating" plants, but I had passed these off as being
akin to ghost stories. Now I was finding myself, at the moment anyway,
living proof of these legends.
        To those of you who are not familiar with these awesome plants, let me
briefly discribe them. The plant as a whole looks quite harmless with
little white flowers. The area of danger is not part of the flower, as
many believe, but rather a part of the leaf. At the end of the leaves
sit a gaping two-sided appendage, brightly colored on the inside and with a
deceivingly innocent appearance. Bordering each is a row of finger-like
projections. When sprung by some means of an electrical charge, these two
halves close together and the fingers interlock. As you may have noticed,
it is not so much the speed at which they close that results in the capture
of its victim as it is the element of surprise involved. Being trapped
by a carnivorous plant is just not the kind of thing I go around expecting
to happen. An interesting point concerning the Venus Fly Trap is the fact
that this area, just off the North and South Carolina coast, is the only
place in the world they are found. And at this moment, I would have just
as soon been in any of those other places.
        Back to my adventure. By now I could barely see light between the
halves of the trap, and this light seemed to be diminishing as time went
by. Was I to become lunch instead of having lunch? So it seemed, for
digestive enzymes were sure to start their job shortly and I would soon

be turned into an empty carcass. This process, as I later found out, actually takes several days, but this isn't my idea of the way to spend a vacation. About the time I was feeling really doomed, I began to hear a loud crunching noise. I pressed up as close as possible to what was now a pinhole of my contact with the outside world. There, right beside my cell was a katydid chomping away at a tuft of grass. I had always heard that katydids had a voracious appetite and would eat almost anything in their path While this one apparently had no particular liking for Venus Fly Traps, he did nip the tip of the trap, breaking off one of the finger-like teeth. This narrow streak of luck is what has enabled me to tell this story today.

Some local flies helped ease my frightened condition, and I was soon eager for a lecture and field trip on what to avoid on my next visit to a marsh. I was shown pitcher plants that dissolve their victims in a pit of digestive juices, and sundews whose "dew-drops" are actually glue and work like natural flypaper (shudder).

I thanked them for the information and headed home. This was sure enough to make me think from there after when I landed on unfamiliar territory. It took a while for me to get over this narrow escape and at times I even considered becoming a "house fly". Eventually the great outdoors won me back, but it had managed to gain my respect. There are things out there that many of us never dream of and one in particular that I can't quit having dreams about.

Story: "View From a Fly's Eye"

SEQUENCE

1. What happened immediately after the fly was about to dig into what he thought was hamburger? (He was surrounded by darkness.)

2. What happens to the parts of the plant as the Venus Fly Trap is sprung? (The two halves close together and the fingers interlock.)

3. What begins to happen to the insect once it is trapped inside the Venus Fly Trap? (The digestive enzymes of the plant begin to work on the insect.)

4. What did the katydid eat after it ate the tuft of grass? (The tip of the trap)

5. Who helped the fly after the katydid made an opening? (Some local flies)

6. What kind of help did the fly get from the local flies after the katydid made an opening in the Venus Fly Trap? (They gave him a lecture and a field trip.)

INFERENCES

1. Choose one of the following to describe the fly's feelings immediately before he became entrapped?
   --frightened
   --hostile
   --eager (correct)
   --cautious

2. The fly had heard stories of fly traps before he encountered this one. To what extent had he believed them up until now? (Not at all. He had passed them off as being akin to ghost stories.)

3. Can Venus Fly Traps be found in California? (No)

4. How do we know the local flies were "experienced" with the area? (They were able to show this fly other dangers.)

5. How does the Venus Fly Trap attract its victims? (By bait that looks like hamburger)

6. How did this fly's view of the great outdoors change as a result of this experience? (He became more cautious.)

MAIN IDEA

1. You are writing a biography of this fly. This story is one chapter in the biography. What would the name of this chapter be? (Judgment of the teacher)

2. If there were to be a lesson learned through this story, what would it be? (Judgment of the teacher)

3. You are writing an item for your school paper. Your information is based on this story. What would your headline be? (Judgment of the teacher)

4. Do you think this story better describes the adventures of a fly with a Venus Fly Trap or does it tell about a typical fly's vacation? (The adventures of a fly with a Venus Fly Trap.)

5. If his story were to be a chapter in a science book you were writing, what would you select as your chapter title? (Judgment of the teacher)

6. Which of the following phrases best describes the main section in this story?
   Why flies get into trouble
   How Nature affects insects
   How a Venus Fly Trap works (correct)
   What happens to a housefly

DETAILS

1. In what state did this story take place? (North Carolina)

2. Why didn't the fly head for a hamburger stand to eat? (He had decided to "live off the land.")

3. What is the color of the flowers on the Venus Fly Trap? (White)

4. What part of the plant is the dangerous part of the Venus Fly Trap? (The leaf)

5. Name another plant which is dangerous to the fly. (The pitcher plant, or the sundew)

6. How does the sundew work? (Like flypaper)

VOCABULARY

1. The story stated "all of a sudden I was hit by an indescribable aroma."
   What does the word <u>aroma</u> mean? (Smell or odor)

2. The story stated that the fly had become a gullible victim of the trap.
   What does the word <u>gullible</u> mean? (Easily fooled)

3. The word <u>carnivorous</u> is used in this story. What is its meaning?
   (Subsisting on nutrients obtained from the breakdown of animal
   protoplasm; flesh-eating)

4. The fly might have been turned into an empty carcass. What does the
   word <u>carcass</u> mean? (A dead body; the decaying or worthless remains of
   a structure)

5. A katydid chomped away at a tuft of grass. What does the word <u>tuft</u> mean?
   (Clump, cluster, or mound)

6. This katydid had a voracious appetite. What does the word <u>voracious</u>
   mean? (Excessively large)

43

THE
READING
GAME

ACTIVITY NO. 6

THE READING MATCH GAME

Purpose

The purpose of the READING MATCH GAME is to provide a relatively easy but competitive exercise to aid in developing students' reading skills. This game allows the slower student to experience success without having his answers labeled "incorrect" or "wrong"; yet, it still issues a challenge for the more advanced students.

Skills

Reading and reading-related skills may be developed through this activity. A particular emphasis may be placed on similarities in word meanings and vocabulary development.

Materials Needed

1. Six "Response Boxes" in which the students may write their answers privately will be needed. The three for one team could be of contrasting colors from those of the opposing team. These boxes may be made of poster board or from shoe boxes.

2. Several blank response sheets (approximately 3" x 5") will be needed for each game. These may be made by cutting sheets of scrap paper into pieces large enough for printing a word or phrase which can be seen by the entire class.

3. Six crayons or large marking pens will be needed for each game.

4. Six small chalk boards, chalk, and erasers may be used in place of the blank response sheets and crayons.

Preparation and Instructional Procedures

1. A selected story should be read by the students.

2. Several statements or phrases to elicit matching responses by team members should be prepared from this selection. Limitless possibilities exist for these statements.

3. Six students are selected to participate--three on each team. The members of each team sit side by side. Teams are at 90 degree angles with each other. All face the class.

4. Both teams are given a statement or phrase, such as "Name one character in this story," and each team member attempts to write the name of a character which he thinks his team members will also name.

5. Upon disclosure of responses (one at a time), each team is awarded 25 points for every match made by any two members of the same team.

6. The team with the highest total at the end of a predetermined number of statements (such as 15) or the team which first reaches a predetermined total (such as 300) wins the game.

Adaptations

1. The entire classroom or participating group can be divided into two teams. Upon the accumulation of each 100 points by each team, the three members of that team change to three others who have not yet participated. Rotating the team members in this fashion creates a higher degree of interest and allows participation by a greater number of students. If a smaller group total is involved (9-15 students) only one new member for each 100 points might be changed.

2. This game could be played following the reading of several stories which may have been evaluated in other ways. Sample statements or phrases might be: "Name an animal in a story we have read this week," or "Name an occupation of someone in one of our reading selections."

3. Word recognition skills may be developed by preparing an exercise to develop these general skills without the use of a specific reading selection. A sample exercise follows the explanation of this activity.

Origin of Activity

THE READING MATCH GAME was based on the former television program "The Match Game." Procedures for this activity were adapted from this television program for educational use in the reading classroom.

Items Provided

The following items are provided in this book and/or in the accompanying Materials Book:

1. Page 45 in this book contains sample statements or phrases which may be used with the READING MATCH GAME without a specific reading selection. These questions may be used to build word recognition skills.

2. Page 47 in the Materials Book contains a READING MATCH GAME design which may be pasted on the outside of the boxes used for this game. Six will be needed.

SAMPLE STATEMENTS OF PHRASES FOR THE READING MATCH GAME

(For use without a specific reading selection)

1. Complete this statement: Reading is _____.
2. Name a story you have recently read.
3. Name a book you have either read or would like to read.
4. Name a character you have read about lately.
5. Write a word that rhymes with flower.
6. Complete this statement: Books are _____.
7. Name a comic strip character.
8. Write a word with a long a sound.
9. Write a word with a short o sound.
10. Write a letter of the alphabet which represents many different sounds.
11. Write a word with the letters -ng at the end.
12. Name something you would like to read during your summer vacation.
13. Name the title of a book you would like to give as a gift to a friend.
14. Name a section of the newspaper.
15. Write a word with the prefix re-.
16. Complete this word: th____.
17. Draw a road sign.
18. Name a reading game besides **THE READING MATCH GAME.**
19. Name an abbreviation commonly used.
20. Name an author.
21. Write a synonym for said.
22. Write a homonym for t-o.
23. Write a word which has a long e sound.
24. Name a book which has had a movie made from it.
25. Write a word which has an /oi/ sound.
26. Write a word with four syllables.
27. Write an antonym for happy.
28. Write a word which has a long o sound.
29. Write a three-letter word.
30. Write a suffix which is commonly used.
31. Write a word which has several different meanings.
32. Write a word which has a short e sound.
33. Name an adjective that describes how you feel about reading.
34. Write one of the first words you learned to read.
35. Write a word which has a long i sound.
36. Name a reason you might look up something in the dictionary.
37. Write a word which has a homonym (other than to).
38. Write a word which has an /au/ sound.
39. Write down how long it usually takes to read a book.
40. Write a word which has a short a sound.
41. Write a word which has a /sh/ sound.
42. Write a word which is an antonym for right.
43. Write a word which has the short i sound.
44. Name a book you might like to buy.
45. Complete this statement: Reading is the most fun when _____.

ACTIVITY NO. 7

Purpose

The purpose of the LINGO exercises is to provide for the students varied opportunities to develop specific reading skills necessary for their reading progress. LINGO exercises allow a game of fun and competitive spirit while learning these reading skills.

Skills

The skills of phonics analysis and structural analysis may be developed through the LINGO exercises. Specific skills and sub-skills are described with each of the six sets of LINGO cards.

Materials Needed

1. One LINGO card per student is needed for each version of LINGO.

2. Twenty-four cover tabs are needed by each student participating.

3. (Optional) Words in the suggested word lists for Sets A-D and meanings for Sets E and F may be written on small cards in order to shuffle for a random selection of items.

Preparation and Instructional Procedures

1. The rules of LINGO are similar to BINGO except that LINGO is used to develop language or reading skills.

2. LINGO is not necessarily related to a specific reading selection and may therefore be played at any time by students.

3. It is necessary for the teacher to know the levels and skills needed by all students before attempting to use these exercises. Depending upon the reading levels and needs of each student, the teacher should form groups to use the sets of LINGO. These sets should be used as an aid in developing the outlined skills and not as an entire program of classroom or individual instruction in these skills. As each student masters the skills of one set of LINGO, he then uses the set next in line of difficulty from Set A to Set F.

4. Ways to win: Before the start of each LINGO exercise, the teacher and students should decide how to win that game. Any possibility decided by the group would be accepted. The following are some possibilities:

    a. Straight LINGO (every square filled in any one row across--do not allow a LINGO in any column down because all columns contain the same items)

b. Four corners (only the squares in each corner need to be filled)

c. Diagonals only (either diagonal)

d. Picture frame (every square in the L and O columns and the top and bottom rows)

e. X (both diagonals must be completed to form an X)

f. + (the N column and the third row both need to be completed to form a +, or plus sign)

g. L shape (all of L column and bottom row)

h. U shape (all of L and O columns and bottom row)

i. Z shape (all of top and bottom rows and diagonal from O to L)

j. Y shape (last three in N column, first square in L and O, second in I and G)

k. T shape (top row and N column)

l. E shape (rows 1, 3, and 5 and·L column)

m. F shape (rows 1 and 3 and L column)

n. H shape (columns L and O and 3rd row)

o. N shape (columns L and O and diagonal from L to O)

p. Any combination of above (such as straight LINGO or four corners)

q. Any other possibility decided upon by group

5. The game of LINGO is designed differently from the traditional BINGO in that each column in BINGO has 15 number possibilities with only five printed on each card (75 total possibilities), whereas LINGO has only 24 total possibilities (one free). In LINGO, each time the teacher calls an item, every student will place a tab on a square somewhere on his card if he knows the correct response. Therefore, the exercises are easier for the students and they encounter each letter combination or word part more frequently.

6. The letter-combinations or word parts selected for each set of LINGO, instructions, the word lists or meaning lists, study sheets (if necessary), and a sample card for each set follow. The design allows each set to be extracted from the guide in order for an aide or a student in the class to direct the exercise for the group selected. The teacher should familiarize all students involved with how the game is played before allowing an aide or another student to direct the exercise.

<u>Items Provided</u>

The following items are provided in this book and/or in the accompanying <u>Materials Book</u>:

1. Six sets of LINGO instructions are included.

    a. Common initial consonant blends (pages 50-51 in this book)

    b. Single vowel letters, vowel digraphs, and vowel diphthongs (pages 52-53)

    c. Various consonant - letter combinations (pages 54-55)

    d. Common derivational suffixes (pages 56-57)

    e. Common prefixes (pages 58-60--page 60 in this book and page 48 in the <u>Materials Book</u> contain a student study sheet for Set E.)

    f. Common roots (pages 61-63--page 63 in this book and page 49 in the <u>Materials Book</u> contain a student study sheet for Set F.)

2. Page 64 in this book and page 50 in the <u>Materials Book</u> provide a blank which may be duplicated to be used with LINGO. Items may be written in with a felt-tipped pen.

3. Page 65 in this book provides a sample LINGO card.

INSTRUCTIONS FOR SET A

1. The squares in Set A of LINGO are filled with the following common initial consonant blends:

   Column L: (Blends ending with <u>l</u>) <u>bl</u>-, <u>gl</u>-, <u>fl</u>-, <u>pl</u>-, <u>cl</u>-

   Column I: (Some blends beginning with <u>s</u>) <u>sk</u>-, <u>sm</u>-, <u>sn</u>-, <u>sp</u>-, <u>st</u>-

   Column N: (Miscellaneous blends) <u>tw</u>-, <u>wh</u>-, <u>sw</u>-, <u>sl</u>-

   Column G: (Some blends ending with <u>r</u>) <u>br</u>-, <u>cr</u>-, <u>dr</u>-, <u>fr</u>-, <u>gr</u>-

   Column O: (Some blends ending with <u>r</u>) <u>pr</u>-, <u>tr</u>-, <u>scr</u>-, <u>str</u>-, <u>thr</u>-

   (Hyphens follow all blends on LINGO cards to indicate that letters would follow in completed words.)

2. Students selected to work with Set A should be those who have basically mastered many of the single initial consonant letters (such as b, c, d, f, g, h, j, l, m, n, p, r, s, t, w). They should have been introduced to the blends included in Set A in regular classroom or individual instruction. This exercise should be used to supplement the teaching of these letter combinations.

3. Distribute cards to those selected students.

4. Decide on the method to win for that game.

5. Call the letter from one column (L, I, N, G, or O) and one word containing one of the blends in that column from the following suggested word list or from other words which students have encountered.

6. The student finds on his card the consonant blend contained in the word just read and places a tab on that blend.

7. This procedure continues until a student wins according to previously decided method.

8. When a student does win, he must read those items which allowed him to win as the teacher checks from the words which have been called. (Optional) To make the exercise more difficult, student should relate a word containing that blend to illustrate his knowledge of it.

9. Continue as desired.

52

WORD LIST FOR SET A

Five examples are provided for each consonant blend. Read the letter for the column, then the word selected. (Example: L - fleet) Mark the column at the right to indicate you have selected a word with that consonant blend. Do not select another word with that same consonant blend until another game is played. Continue until a student wins.

Column	Consonant Blend	Suggested Examples	Others	Check
L	bl- gl- fl- pl- cl-	black, blue, blouse, bleak, blow glass, glue, glide, glee, glow flow, flower, fleet, fly, flea plea, pleat, plow, plate, plum clock, club, climb, clay, clue		
I	sk- sm- sn- sp- st-	sky, ski, skull, skunk, skirt smell, smile, small, smoke, smart snail, snap, snake, snore, snow spell, spill, speak, spoke, spine stop, stuck, stick, stove, stock		
N	tw- wh- sw- sl-	twine, tweed, twelve, twice, twin where, when, why, which, what sweet, switch, swing, swim, swell slide, sleep, slip, sled, sling		
G	br- cr- dr- fr- gr-	brown, bright, breath, bride, brick cream, crow, cry, cradle, crib draw, drop, drum, dress, drive from, fry, free, French, friend gravy, groom, great, grow, grind		
O	pr- tr- scr- str- thr-	preach, pray, print, prize, prison trip, tray, tree, try, trim scream, scroll, screen, scratch, scrub string, stripe, street, stream, straw three, throat, thread, throne, through		

Note: Sample words added must not contain another consonant blend also included in the same column.

1. The squares in Set B of LINGO are filled with the following single vowel letters, vowel digraphs, and vowel diphthongs.

   Column L: (Single vowel letters--one spelling of the conventionally named short vowels) a, e, i, o, u

   Column I: (Some common vowel digraphs) ew, au, aw, oo, ei

   Column N: (Common vowel diphthongs) ow, ou, oi, oy

   Column G: (Vowel digraphs commonly found within syllables) ai, ea, ee, oa, ui

   Column O: (Vowel digraphs commonly found at the end of syllables) ie, oe, ue, ay, ey

   (Hyphens are omitted from cards for Set B because of the varieties of occurrences of these vowels in completed words.)

2. Students selected to work with Set B should be those who have basically mastered many of the single initial consonant letters, those who have begun mastery of the consonant blends. Before using this exercise, the students should have been introduced to these vowel letter combinations in regular classroom or individual instruction. This exercise should be used to supplement the teaching of these vowel letters and letter combinations.

3. Distribute cards to those selected students.

4. Decide on the method to win for that game.

5. Call the letter from one column (L, I, N, G, or O) and one word containing one of the vowel letters or combinations in that column from the suggested word list or from other words which students have encountered.

6. The student finds on his card the vowel letter or combination contained in the word just read and places a tab on that square.

7. This procedure continues until a student wins according to the previously decided method.

8. When a student does win, he must read those items which allowed him to win as the teacher checks from the words which have been called. (Optional) To make the exercise more difficult, student should relate a word containing that vowel letter or combination to illustrate his knowledge of it.

9. Continue as desired.

WORD LIST FOR SET B

Several examples are provided for each vowel letter or letter combination. Read the letter for the column, then the word selected. (Example: G - boat) Mark the column at the right to indicate you have selected a word with that vowel. Do not select another word with that vowel until another game is played. Continue until a student wins.

Column	Vowel	Suggested Examples Others	Check
L	a	bat, hat, fan, mad, than	
	e	bet, red, pet, met, then	
	i	bit, hit, pin, fit, lip	
	o	hot, mop, plod, Don, lot	
	u	hut, cut, fun, up, sun	
I	ew	few, sew, view, pew, grew	
	au	applaud, caught, taught	
	aw	saw, jaw, law, raw, slaw, flaw	
	oo	food, book, look, foot, hook	
	ei	receive, either, seize, deceive	
N	ow	plow, crowd, bow, glower	
	ou	house, blouse, louse, out	
	oi	toil, oil, void, foil, hoist	
	oy	boy, toy, enjoy, employ	
G	ai	mail, tail, pail, detail, frail	
	ea	meat, eat, pleat, heat, read	
	ee	meet, feet, deed, reed, weed	
	oa	boat, float, groan, moan	
	ui	suit, fruit, juice	
O	ie	pie, tie, lie, replied	
	oe	shoe, hoe, toe	
	ue	blue, Sue, true, flue	
	ay	way, say, day, May, hay, pray	
	ey	they, whey, prey	

1. The squares in Set C of LINGO are filled with the following various consonant-letter combinations.

   <u>Column L:</u> (Some common final consonant digraphs) -<u>th</u>, -<u>ch</u>, -<u>sh</u>, -<u>ng</u>, -<u>gh</u>

   <u>Column I:</u> (Some consonant letter combinations with one silent letter) <u>kn</u>-, <u>wr</u>-, <u>gn</u>-, <u>pn</u>-, -<u>bt</u>

   <u>Column N:</u> (Some common initial consonant digraphs) <u>ch</u>-, <u>sh</u>-, <u>th</u>-, <u>ph</u>-

   <u>Column G:</u> (Three difficult single consonants and two common final consonant blends) -<u>x</u>, <u>z</u>-, <u>y</u>-, -<u>cks</u>, -<u>ld</u>

   <u>Column O:</u> (Some common final consonant blends) -<u>sk</u>, -<u>sp</u>, -<u>st</u>, -<u>nd</u>, -<u>rt</u>

   (Hyphens are appropriately placed on LINGO cards to indicate where letters would be placed in completed words.)

2. Students selected to work with Set C should be those who have basically mastered the skills described in Sets A and B. Before using this exercise the students selected should have been introduced to these consonant letter combinations in regular classroom or individual instruction. This exercise should be used to supplement this instruction.

3. Distribute cards to those selected students.

4. Decide on the method to win for that game.

5. Call the letter from one column (<u>L</u>, <u>I</u>, <u>N</u>, <u>G</u>, or <u>O</u>) and one word containing one of the consonant-letter combinations in that column from the suggested word list or from other words which students have encountered.

6. The student finds on his card the consonant-letter combination contained in the word just read and places a tab on that square.

7. This procedure continues until a student wins according to the previously decided method.

8. When a student does win, he must read those items which allowed him to win as the teacher checks from the words which have been called. (Optional) To make the exercise more difficult, student should relate a word containing that consonant-letter combination to illustrate his knowledge of it.

9. Continue as desired.

WORD LIST FOR SET C

Several examples are provided for each consonant-letter combination.
Read the letter for the column, then the word selected. (Example: 0 -
fist) Mark the column at the right to indicate you have selected a word
with that consonant-letter combination. Do not select another word with
that consonant-letter combination until another game is played. Continue
until a student wins.

Column	Consonant Letter Combination	Suggested Examples Others	Check
L	-th -ch -sh -ng -gh	with, breath, path, bath church, each, which, peach fish, dish, hash, wish, rash sing, song, hung, wrong, king cough, rough, tough, trough	
I	kn- wr- gn- pn- -bt	knit, knife, knight, knee, knock write, wrong, wreath, wrench gnat, gnaw, gnash, gnarl, gnome pneumonia, pneumatic debt, doubt	
N	ch- sh- th- ph-	church, cheap, chair, child show, shy, shine, shoe, shield the, then, there, these, thou phone, physics, pharmacy	
G	-x z- y- -cks -ld	box, fix, fox, six, tax, wax zebra, zoo, zenith, zoom, zipper yellow, yet, young, yes, yield socks, picks, tacks, packs hold, held, build, bold, cold	
O	-sk -sp -st -nd -rt	risk, flask, ask, frisk wasp, grasp, lisp, rasp fist, must, trust, cost hand, find, pond, end heart, hurt, part, start	

INSTRUCTIONS FOR SET D

1. The squares in Set D of LINGO are filled with the following common derivational suffixes.

   Column L: -ly, -est, -er, -ar, -or

   Column I: -en, -al, -tion, -ble, -ness

   Column N: -ant, -ent, -ance, -ence

   Column G: -ment, -ward, -like, -teen, -ious

   Column O: -ic, -ish, -age, -ful, -less

   (Hyphens precede the suffixes on the LINGO cards to indicate where other syllables would be in completed words.)

2. Students selected to work with Set D should have mastered the skills involved in Sets A-C.

3. Distribute cards to those selected students.

4. Decide on the method to win for that game.

5. Call the letter from one column (L, I, N, G, or O) and one word containing one of the suffixes in that column from the suggested word list or from other words which students have encountered.

6. The student finds on his card the suffix contained in the word just read and places a tab on that square.

7. This procedure continues until a student wins according to the previously decided method.

8. When a student does win, he must read those items which allowed him to win as the teacher checks from the words which have been called. (Optional) to make the exercise more difficult, student should relate a word containing that suffix to illustrate his knowledge of it.

9. Continue as desired.

WORD LIST FOR SET D

Several examples are provided for each suffix. Read the letter for the column, then the word selected. (Example: I - <u>table</u>) Mark the column at the right to indicate you have selected a word with that suffix. Do not select another word with that same suffix until another game is played. Continue until a student wins.

Column	Suffix	Suggested Examples Others	Check
L	- ly -est - er - ar - or	kingly, swiftly, nicely finest, fattest, greatest farmer, preacher, lawyer, dollar, collar, scholar doctor, educator, furor	
I	- en - al -tion -ble -ness	darken, straighten, weaken dental, portal, medical nation, portion, section table, wobble, tremble kindness, likeness, thoroughness	
N	- ant - ent - ance -ence	assistant, expectant, operant present, different, consistent disturbance, performance, resonance difference, presence, pestilence	
G	-ment -ward - like -teen -ious	acknowledgement, parchment, advertisement downward, forward, upward lifelike, childlike, warlike sixteen, thirteen, eighteen precious, pretentious, facetious	
O	-ic -ish - age -ful - less	panic, comic, psychic boyish, childish, devilish mileage, pilgrimage, homage thankful, thoughtful, spoonful childless, friendless, motherless	

INSTRUCTIONS FOR SET E

1. The squares in Set E of LINGO are filled with the following common prefixes.

   Column L: a(d)-, anti-, bi-, co(n)-, de-

   Column I: dis-, e(x)-, for(e)-, in-, inter-

   Column N: mal-, mis-, non-, post-

   Column G: pre-, pro-, re-, semi-, su(b)-

   Column O: tel(e), trans-, tri-, un-, uni-

   (Hyphens follow prefixes on LINGO cards to indicate that other syllable(s) would follow in completed words. Parentheses enclosing letters indicate that that letter may either be included or omitted in the spelling when the prefix is added to a root.)

2. Students selected to work with Set E of LINGO should have mastered the skills necessary for Sets A-D. Before Set E is used, the students involved should have a full understanding of the meaning and function of a prefix. They should also know how spellings of words are changed when a prefix such as ex- is added to a root such as mit (emit). Since this exercise requires that the students know the meaning of the prefix rather than simply recognize it in a word, a study sheet should be given to each student of this group but should not be used during an actual LINGO game.

3. Distribute cards to those selected students.

4. Decide upon the method to win for that game.

5. Call out one column letter (L, I, N, G, or O) and the meaning of one of the prefixes in the list for that column. (Example G - half) Do not give an example of a word containing that prefix.

6. The student finds on his card the prefix corresponding to the meaning given and places a tab on that prefix.

7. This procedure continues until a student wins according to the previously decided method.

8. When a student does win, he must read those prefixes corresponding to the given meanings. (Optional) The student may further be asked to give a word containing that prefix or give a meaning of that prefix.

9. Continue as desired.

MEANING LIST FOR SET E

The literal meaning for each prefix is provided below. Read the letter
for the column, then the meaning of the prefix selected. (Example: L -
two). Mark the column at the right to indicate you have selected that
prefix and meaning. Do not give an example of a word containing the
prefix itself. If a prefix has two meanings, read both. Continue until
a student wins.

Column	Prefix	Meaning(s)	Check
L	a(d)- anti- bi- co(n)- de-	to, toward against two with, together down, from	
I	dis- e(x)- for(e)- in- inter-	apart, away out of, from beforehand not, into among, between	
N	mal- mis- non- post-	bad wrong no, not after	
G	pre- pro- re- semi- su(b)	before forward back, again half under	
O	tel(e)- trans- tri- un- uni-	far off across, over three not, opposite of one	

Prefixes	Meaning	Examples
a(d)-	to, toward	adjacent, accept, attend, appear, adventure
anti-	against	antisocial, anticlimax, antiwar, anti-American
bi-	two	bicycle, biplane, bimodal
co(n)-	with, together	cooperate, confer, copilot, company, contain
de-	down, from	descend, depart, detain, detract
dis-	apart, away	digress, dissolve, dissimilar, dismiss
e(x)-	out of, from	exit, emit, extend, expel, exclude
for(e)-	beforehand	forewarn, forecast, foretell
in-	not, into	intolerable, inconsistent, include, import
inter-	among, between	intersect, intervene
mal-	bad	malfunction, malodorous, malady
mis-	wrong	mistake, misnomer
non-	no, not	nontoxic, nonexistent
post-	after	postscript, postpone
pre-	before	preview, prepare, prenatal
pro-	forward	project, provide
re-	back, again	repaint, redecorate, return, report, rewrite
semi-	half	semiannual, semimonthly
su(b)-	under	submarine, suffer, suppress
tel(e)	far off	telescope, telephone, telegraph
trans-	across, over	transfer, transport
tri-	three	tricycle, tricolor, tripod
un-	not, opposite of	unfastened, undecided, undo
uni-	one	unit, unicycle, unicorn

INSTRUCTIONS FOR SET F

1. The squares in Set F of LINGO are filled with the following common roots:

   Column L: -astron-, -auto-, -bio-, -chron-, -clud(e)-

   Column I: -duc(e)-, -fact-, -form-, -geo-, -graph-

   Column N:*   -aqua-, -spec(t)-, -mini-, -scrib(e)-

   Column G: -hydro-, -meter-, -micro-, -mit(t)-, -olog-

   Column O: -phob-, -phon-, -port-, -scop(e)-, -vent-

   (Hyphens are placed before and after roots in LINGO cards to indicate that syllables may be placed before and after these roots in completed words. Parentheses enclosing letters indicate that that letter may either be included or omitted in the spelling when a suffix is added to that root.)
   *Roots in Row N have meanings of some roots in other columns.

2. Students selected to work with Set F of LINGO should have mastered the skills necessary for Sets A-E. Before Set F is used, the students involved should have a full understanding of the meaning and function of a root. They should also know how spellings of words are changed when a root is joined with affixes. (Example: telescopic) Since this exercise requires that the students know the meaning of the root rather than simply recognize it in a word, a study sheet should be given to each student of this group but should not be used during an actual LINGO game.

3. Distribute cards to those selected students.

4. Decide upon the method to win for that game.

5. Call out one column letter (L, I, N, G, or O) and the meaning of one of the roots in the list for that column. Do not give an example of a word containing that root.

6. The student finds on his card the root corresponding to the meaning given and places a tab on that root.

7. This procedure continues until a student wins according to the previously decided method.

8. When a student does win, he must read those roots corresponding to the given meanings. (Optional) The student may further be asked to give a word containing that root or give a meaning of that root.

9. Continue as desired.

MEANING LIST FOR SET F

The literal meaning for each root is provided below. Read the letter for
the column, then the meaning of the root selected. (Example: O - <u>fear</u>)
Mark the column at the right to indicate you have selected that root and
meaning. Do not give an example of a word containing the root itself.
If a root has two meanings, read both. Continue until a student wins.

Column	Root	Meaning(s)	Check
L,	-astron-	stars	
	-auto-	self	
	-bio-	life	
	-chron-	time	
	-clud(e)-	close	
I	-duc(e)-	lead	
	-fact-	do, make	
	-form-	shape	
	-geo-	earth	
	-graph-	write	
N	-aqua-	water	
	-spec(t)-	look	
	-mini-	small	
	-scrib(e)-	write	
G	-hydro-	water	
	-meter-	measure	
	-micro-	small	
	-mit(t)-	send	
	-olog-	study of	
O	-phob-	fear	
	-phon-	sound	
	-port-	carry	
	-scop(e)-	see	
	-vent-	come	

64

Roots	Meaning	Examples
-aqua-	water	aquatic, aquarium, aquaplane, aquamarine
-astron-	stars	astronomy, astronaut
-auto-	self	automatic, autobiography, autograph, automobile
-bio-	life	biology, biography
-chron-	time	chronological, chronicle
-clud(e)-	close	include, recluse
-duc(e)-	lead	induce, conduct
-fact-	do, make	manufacture, facile
-form-	shape	transform, reform, formation
-geo-	earth	geography, geology
-graph-	write	autograph, photograph, biography
-hydro-	water	hydrant, hydraulic, hydroelectric
-meter-	measure	meter, speedometer, micrometer, thermometer
-micro-	small	microscope, microphone, micrometer, microbe
-mini-	small	miniskirt, minimum, miniature, minimize
-mit(t)-	send	permit, transmit, omit, submit
-olog-	study of	geology, biology, graphology
-phob-	fear	phobia, claustrophobia
-phon-	sound	phone, telephone, megaphone, phonics, microphone
-port-	carry	portable, transport, import, export, report
-scop(e)-	see	telescope, microscope
-scrib(e)-	write	inscribe, prescribe, subscribe
-spec(t)-	look	spectacles, inspect, spectator
-vent-	come	vent, convention, invent

65

LINGO

FREE

L	I	N	G	O
anti-	for(e)-	mal-	pre-	tel(e)-
bi-	in-	mis-	semi-	tri-
co(n)-	inter-	**FREE**	re-	un-
de-	e(x)-	post-	pro-	trans-
a(d)-	dis-	non-	su(b)-	uni-

READING
BASEBALL

ACTIVITY NO. 8

Purpose

The purpose of the activity READING BASEBALL is to promote interest and enthusiasm in the development of students' necessary reading and reading-related skills by capitalizing on the students' interest in the sport of baseball. The activity is also designed to challenge students of both extremes of reading ability by allowing a choice of easy or difficult questions to answer.

Skills

Literal and inferential comprehension skills may be developed through this activity.

Materials Needed

1. (Optional) A transparency of a baseball diamond with places for the score, innings, and outs for each team may be used. (The form for this transparency is included in the **Materials Book**.) The same form may be drawn on the chalkboard instead of using a transparency.

2. (For adaptation of activity) A READING BASEBALL poster may be made from a 22" x 28" sheet of poster paper. (A form for this poster is shown at the end of this explanation.)

Preparation and Instructional Procedures

1. A selected story should be read by the students.

2. Questions must be prepared on four levels of difficulty from the selection read. (For the adaptation of the game, questions need not be of varying difficulty.)

3. The class or participating group is divided into two teams (Team A and Team B).

4. As a student "steps up to bat," he tells the "pitcher" (teacher or director) whether he wishes a "single", "double", "triple", or "homerun" question, knowing that these questions vary in difficulty depending upon how far he will be able to advance on the bases.

5. If the question is answered correctly, the student advances to the base selected. (This is drawn with an X on the chalkboard or a penny is placed on the appropriate base on the transparency.)

6. If the question is answered incorrectly, the student makes an out for his team.

7. The activity proceeds until the predetermined number of innings have been played and one team wins.

Adaptation of Activity

An adaptation of the activity requires a READING BASEBALL board to be made which allows the student to twirl a consequence rather than select one. (See form for board at end of explanation.) Procedures for this adaptation are as follows:

1. The "batter" twirls the bat on the READING BASEBALL board.

2. If the arrow at the end of the bat points to "single", "double", "triple", or "home-run", the student is given an opportunity to respond to a question prepared by the teacher.

3. If the student answers this question correctly, he advances to that base.

4. If he answers this question incorrectly, he does not make an out but sits down and the next batter takes his turn.

5. If the student twirls "strike", "foul ball", or "ball", he continues twirling until four balls or three strikes are accumulated, or until he twirls another consequence.

6. Activity proceeds until the predetermined number of innings have been played and one team wins.

Items Provided

The following items are provided in this book and/or in the accompanying Materials Book:

1. Page 69 in this book shows a sample READING BASEBALL board.

2. Page 70 in this book and page 51 in the Materials Book provide a form which may be used to make a transparency for READING BASEBALL.

3. Pages 71-72 in this book and pages 52-55 in the Materials Book contain a sample story which may be used for this game.

4. Pages 73-75 in this book contain questions for the sample story.

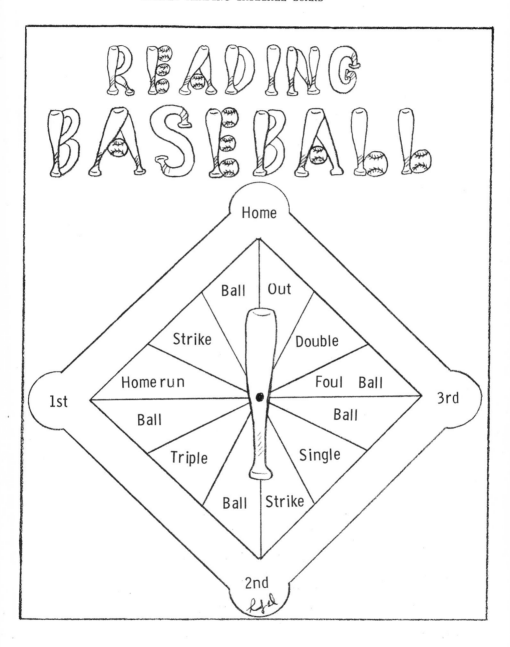

READING BASEBALL

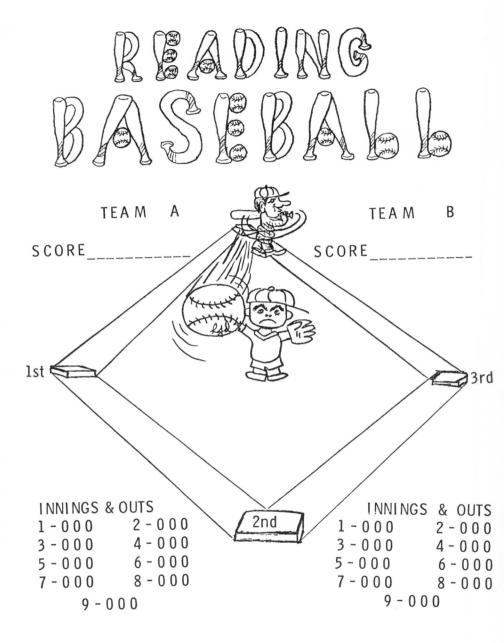

TEAM   A

SCORE_____

TEAM   B

SCORE_____

1st

3rd

2nd

INNINGS & OUTS
1 - 0 0 0   2 - 0 0 0
3 - 0 0 0   4 - 0 0 0
5 - 0 0 0   6 - 0 0 0
7 - 0 0 0   8 - 0 0 0
    9 - 0 0 0

INNINGS & OUTS
1 - 0 0 0   2 - 0 0 0
3 - 0 0 0   4 - 0 0 0
5 - 0 0 0   6 - 0 0 0
7 - 0 0 0   8 - 0 0 0
    9 - 0 0 0

A MAN OF PEACE

by Douglas Norman

The crowd which had gathered around the field gasped. They had come from nearby Redhill, England, to see a demonstration of the new explosive called dynamite, but they had expected nothing like this.

The distinguished looking man standing alone near the center of the field said that he would set a stick of the explosive afire. The people shook their heads and fell further back. This man Nobel must surely be mad. Look at the many horrible accidents that had occured when nitro-glycerin was heated, or even shaken. And did not this new dynamite contain nitroglycerin as an ingredient?

The distinguished looking man was, they knew, Alfred Nobel. He was the world's largest manufacturer of nitroglycerin, and now he was demon-strating a new explosive which he said was much safer than nitroglycerin.

An assistant carried a stick of the dynamite out to a small mudbank and plunged its bottom into the soft earth. Another assistant handed Alfred Nobel a flaming torch. He advanced slowly until he stood before the stick of explosive. He paused a moment; then he swung the flaming head of the torch down to the dynamite. The crowd waited. Would there be an explosion? Some turned their heads aside. The dynamite flickered, sputtered briefly and then flared into a flame smaller than Nobel's torch. A murmur passed through the crowd. Nobel faced the crowd and held up his hand for silence.

"Ladies and Gentlemen, I believe that this demonstration proves that my new explosive, dynamite, is so safe that it will not explode even when it is exposed to searing heat, but will merely burn slowly."

Before he could say more a young man with the blond hair of the Swedish rushed up to him.

"Mr. Nobel, are you sure that you want to go through with the rest of the demonstration? Burning a single stick is one thing, but this next---."

Alfred Nobel turned to the young man.

"Do not worry, Carl. The only way to explode dynamite is to use a fuse and detonator."

He paused.

"This is not nitroglycerin, Carl. Now prepare our next demonstration."

In a few minutes the crowd saw the figure of the assistant at the top of a huge boulder 60 feet high which stood near the end of the field. In his arms he carried not a single stick but an entire case of dynamite. Nobel again faced the crowd. In it he knew were the leaders of the mining and quarrying industries of England. Upon what he was doing depended the lives of many of their employees who would be killed of injuries the coming year because they were forced to use an explosive like nitroglycerin in their work--an explosive that was extremely dangerous to use.

He spoke.

"To prove that my new explosive will not explode even when it receives a severe jolt, my assistant will hurl an entire case of dynamite from a high rock near the opposite end of the field."

The mining leaders looked at each other and **again** shook their heads. This was too much to believe! Nitroglycerin exploded even when jarred slightly. They remembered how the steamer <u>European</u> was blown to bits off the coast of Panama when its cargo of nitroglycerin exploded, or how a warehouse in San Francisco where it was stored was destroyed by an explosion. Some remembered the story of how an explosion shattered Nobel's first factory for the manufacturing of nitroglycerin. One of the persons killed in that disaster was Alfred Nobel's younger, gifted brother.

They could see why this man Nobel so desired to invent a safer explosive but they could not bring themselves to believe that the new dynamite could be treated like ordinary sticks of wood.

"Stand back. He's going to drop it."

The assistant raised the wooden case above his head. The crowd tensed. Some moved further back. The assistant raised his arms. The box fell in what seemed like an eternal arc. Then it struck the base of the boulder. The box shattered into pieces. Sticks of dynamite flew in many directions. But there was no explosion!

Alfred Nobel received the congratulations of the crowd quietly. He had found an explosive much safer to use than any man had ever known. His invention would save the lives of countless men who dug rock and coal out of the ground. For this he was happy. But still a vague uneasiness troubled him. In his mind he saw his father lying in his bed, paralyzed. He had had a part in building the first factory that made nitroglycerin. Alfred remembered the day when his family received the news that the factory had been destroyed by an explosion and that, worse, his younger brother had lost his life in the blast. He saw his father overwrought with grief, stricken down, to be crippled for the rest of his life.

Another thing also troubled Alfred Nobel. He was a pacifist, a person who does not believe in war. Yet in his heart he knew that he had created an explosive that would **make** war much the easier to wage.

"Have I invented something that will do the world great harm?" he asked himself as he watched the crowd leaving the field after the demonstration. "Will I be the cause of greater wars than the world has ever seen?"

He could not bring himself to believe this. Afterwards he wrote to a friend: "My factories may end war sooner than the peace congresses. The day when two army corps will be able to destroy each other in one second, all civilized nations will recoil from war and disband their armies."

Throughout his lifetime Alfred Nobel worked for the dream of a world without war, a world that would never turn the inventions he had perfected to help people into instruments of destruction. The idea of an enduring peace inspired him all of his life. When he became old he was troubled by the thought of what to do with his huge fortune. He had amassed $9,000,000 from the manufacture of explosives, but he had only one thought. How could he help the cause of world peace?

The world was to find Alfred Nobel's answer to that question in his will. In it he wrote: "I have left the whole of my estate for the forming of a fund, the interest on which shall be awarded for the most important discoveries or achievements in the wide field of knowledge and progress."

"It is my wish that persons be especially considered who are successful (in furthering) the inauguration of a European peace tribunal."

Alfred Nobel might have been remembered as the inventor of dynamite. Instead, because of his hatred of war and violence, we remember him as the man who gave his name to one of the **most** distinguished awards it is possible for man to receive---the Nobel Peace Prize.

SAMPLE QUESTIONS FOR READING BASEBALL

Story: "A Man of Peace"

SINGLE

1. Who was the Man of Peace? (Alfred Nobel)

2. In what country did this story take place? (England)

3. Who was the world's largest manufacturer of nitroglycerin? (Alfred Nobel)

4. In which of the following places was this experiment conducted?
   --inside a building
   --in an open field (correct)
   --at a lake

5. Who was the inventor of dynamite? (Alfred Nobel)

6. How much money did Nobel accumulate from his manufacture of explosives? ($9 million)

7. What happened when the dynamite was burned? (It flickered, sputtered, burned in a small flame very slowly, then went out.)

8. What happened when the dynamite was dropped? (It flew in many directions, but there was no explosion.)

9. What happens when nitroglycerin is shaken? (It explodes.)

10. What happens when nitroglycerin is heated? (It explodes.)

DOUBLE

1. What two experiments did Nobel do with his new dynamite? (He burned it and dropped it.)

2. How much dynamite was dropped in the second experiment? (A case)

3. Why did Carl not want Nobel to continue with the second demonstration? (Carl was too frightened.)

4. Who actually conducted these experiments? (Nobel and his assistants)

5. How did the crowd regard Nobel while he was testing his new dynamite? (They thought he must surely be mad.)

6. How had Nobel's father been affected by nitroglycerin? (He was crippled because of it.)

7. How had Nobel's brother been affected by nitroglycerin? (He was killed because of it.)

8. In what building was Nobel's brother killed? (In the first factory for the manufacturing of nitroglycerin)

9. Why was the steamer _European_ blown to bits off the coast of Panama? (It had nitroglycerin aboard which exploded.)

10. What one ingredient of dynamite was mentioned in this story? (Nitroglycerin)

TRIPLE

1. What is a pacifist? (One who does not believe in war)

2. Who were some of the people in the crowd? (Leaders of the mining and quarrying industries)

3. Why were these leaders interested in the outcome of the experiment? (Dynamite could be used in their work instead of the dangerous nitroglycerin.)

4. At which two of the following specific places were the experiments done?
   --a mudbank (correct)
   --a lake
   --a boulder (correct)
   --a pasture
   --a stadium
   --an open road

5. What did the story say was the only way to explode dynamite? (With a fuse and detonator)

6. What word would describe the mood of the crowd watching the experiments? (Tense, anxious, etc.)

7. Contrast the qualities of dynamite and nitroglycerin. (Nitroglycerin will explode if shaken or dropped; dynamite won't.)

8. How could Nobel's experiment make war easier to wage? (By making it possible to destroy each other quickly)

9. How could Nobel's discovery affect peace? (By making it possible to destroy one another in one second, armies may recoil from war.)

10. How did Nobel's fortune affect peace? (By using it for the award of the Nobel Peace Prize thus promoting action for peace)

HOMERUN (Correctness of answers will depend upon the judgment of the teache

1. What do we know about the bravery of Alfred Nobel?

2. What were Nobel's feelings regarding the past use of nitroglycerin?

3. Discuss Nobel's feelings regarding the success of his discovery?

4. Discuss the belief of the crowd before the experiments with dynamite?

5. Discuss the belief of the crowd after the experiments with dynamite?

6. Discuss the excitement which the crowd displayed following the experiments?

7. What was Nobel's primary wish for the future of the world?

8. Why do we remember Nobel more for the Nobel Peace Prize rather than as the inventor of dynamite?

9. How do you think Nobel's father might have felt regarding these experiments

10. How might this invention have affected the pacifists in the world?

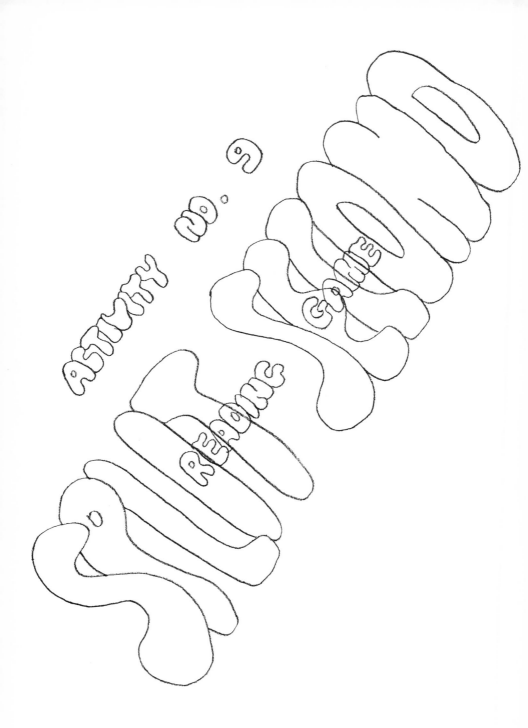

ACTIVITY NO. 9

SUPERSOUND

READING GAME

SPLIT SECOND READING GAME

Purpose

The purpose of SPLIT SECOND READING GAME is to promote interest and enthusiasm in the development of the students' necessary reading and reading-related skills through a thought-provoking and competitive activity.

Skills

General skills relating to vocabulary development may be enhanced through this activity.

Materials Needed

1. A way to portray the items to be used in this game is needed. The most practical way for a group to watch and participate is for the items to be projected via transparencies (or an opaque projector). In this manner the entire group can see the items at once. The chalkboard may be used; however, too much time is usually consumed if items are written and erased each round. Poster boards could be used; however, they tend to become cumbersome. If a very small group is participating, items may be typed or written on large index cards.

2. A way to portray the amount accumulated by each individual team is needed. This may be written on the chalkboard by a student designated to keep the running scores. Playmoney may be used; however, a disadvantage is that scores may not be readily viewed by the audience.

3. A way to portray the number of questions each player needs to answer in the final round is needed. Again, this may be written on the chalkboard, or small number cards may be used.

4. A stopwatch or clock with a second hand will be needed.

Preparation and Instructional Procedures

1. Information on which categories and items are based should be decided by teacher and students. They may come from the vocabulary involved in any phase of study in which the students are or have been involved. (See examples of various types of categories and items in the Materials Book.)

2. Categories and items should be prepared. This is done by selecting one broad category with three items, questions, statements to be completed, etc.

3. Divide the class into three teams. One member from each team will participate at a time. Rotation of members will occur as teacher or students desire. In this manner, all students are either directly participating or "rooting" for their team member.

4. The first part of the game consists of two rounds, each ending upon the completion of previously determined number of categories (i.e., 6-12 categories, or 1-2 pages of the sample materials at the end). Round 1 is followed by Round 2 with the only difference being the amount of money being awarded for each correct response. (See #9.) Round 2 is followed by the Final Round explained below.

ROUNDS 1 and 2

5. Players are read the category and the explanation of what they are to look for in each of the three items. They are then shown the three items.

6. When the items are flashed on the screen, the time is begun. A total of 30 seconds (or other previously determined period of time) is allowed.

7. As the student desires to respond, he raises his hand, is acknowledged by the director, then gives his answer. Student must have his answer in mind before he raises his hand. If his response is not immediate, he loses his chance to attempt to answer. This prevents the student from raising his hand then taking time to decide on his answer, to decide on the easiest item, etc.

8. Each player may attempt only one response. Following the response of the first player, either of the two remaining may raise his hand; then the last player is given an opportunity to respond. All attempts must be made within the 30-second time period. (For items left unanswered, see #10.) If a player's response is incorrect, the director indicates so at that time in order for the remaining players to know that item is still available to be answered.

9. In rounds one and two, money is awarded for each player responding correctly as follows:

	Round 1	Round 2
Correct responses given by all three players	$ 5	$10
Two correct responses given	$10	$25
Only one correct response given	$25	$50

10. If an item is left unanswered correctly, rather than telling the correct answer, the director of the game throws the question out to the class. The class members respond by show of hands. The director calls on the first person whose hand he sees raised. If that person is correct, he adds one dollar to his team's total. If incorrect, director continues calling on class members until the question is answered or no hands are raised. He then relates the correct answer.

FINAL ROUND

11. Before this round is begun, players are designated a specific number of questions which they must answer correctly. The player with the highest accumulated total must answer only three questions, the next highest four, and the lowest five.

12. Steps 5, 6, and 7 are repeated.

13. This round differs, however, in that when a player's hand-raise is acknowledged, he may continue to answer as many of the three items as he can get right as long as his answers are immediate. If a time lapse of more than 5 seconds passes, another player gets his turn to respond.

14. This round is continued until one player has correctly answered his designated number of questions. That player and his team are declared the winner.

Origin of the Activity

SPLIT SECOND READING GAME was based on the currently popular television program "Split Second." Procedures for this activity were adapted from this television program for educational use in the reading classroom.

Items Provided

The following items are provided in this book or in the accompanying Materials Book:

1. Pages 80-99 in this book contain the teacher's key for 120 sets of categories and items which may be used in SPLIT SECOND READING GAME. An attempt is made to repeat many categories such as "Homonyms" to aid in long-term learning. An attempt is also made to graduate the difficulty of the items, although every category is not specifically more difficult than the preceding one. Items are numbered only for organizational purposes, not to reflect level of difficulty.

   It is suggested that one to two rounds be played each week, with some of the interim time used for periodic discussions of some of the difficulties which the rounds have revealed.

2. Pages 56-75 in the Materials Book contain pages which correspond to the 20 pages in this book. These pages contain only the items which the students are to see in order to play the game. They are typed in large type and are prepared for use with an overhead or opaque projector.

1. **SIMILES**
   A simile is a comparison of two things using <u>like</u> or <u>as</u>. Complete
   the following similes with the names of birds or animals.

   blind as a _____   (bat)
   as the _____ flies   (crow)
   eyes like a _____   (hawk)

2. **FAMOUS PAIRS**
   Many words occur in pairs. Complete each of the following pairs.

   Dick and _____   (Jane)
   Rowen and _____   (Martin)
   Sanford and _____   (Son)

3. **PARTS OF SPEECH**
   The following are three parts of speech with the vowel letters omitted.
   What are they?

   ntrjctn   (interjection)
   djctv   (adjective)
   prpstn   (preposition)

4. **EXPRESSIONS - ANIMALS**
   There are many names of animals in various expressions which we use
   frequently. Fill in the following blanks with names of animals.

   eager _____   (beaver)
   _____pecked   (hen)
   road_____   (hog)

5. **SN-**
   Each of the following phrases defines a word which begins with <u>sn-</u>.
   What are they?

   a reptile   (snake)
   a rough breathing noise during sleep   (snore)
   the nose of a beast   (snout)

6. **HOMONYMS**
   Homonyms are words which sound alike but are spelled differently.
   Spell a homonym for the following words.

   I   (eye, aye)
   in   (inn)
   be   (bee)

   The items on this page to be shown to the students are typed

   # IN   LARGE   TYPE in the <u>Materials Book</u> for

   use with an overhead or opaque projector.

7. APOSTROPHES

If an apostrophe were placed in a particular place in the following words, they would be different words altogether. What would they be?

id   (I'd)

cant   (can't)

wont   (won't)

8. NUMBER WORDS

The following definitions have to do with numbers. What are they?

four singers   (quartet)

group of twelve   (dozen)

three-sided figure   (triangle)

9. EXPRESSIONS - WEATHER

Words pertaining to weather occur in various expressions. Fill in the blanks with words pertaining to weather.

right as _____   (rain)

soft as a _____   (cloud)

it never _____ but it pours   (rains)

10. COMPOUND WORDS

A compound word is a combination of two different words. The first part of the following compound words is <u>sun</u>. From the following definitions provide the complete word.

a day of the week   (Sunday)

light from the sun   (sunlight, sunshine)

descent of the sun below the horizon (sunset, sundown)

11. HOMONYMS

Homonyms are words which sound alike but are spelled differently. Spell a homonym for the following words.

ate   (eight)

road   (rode)

hear   (here)

12. PERIOD

By adding a period to some words, they become an abbreviation. If a period were added to each of these words, what would the abbreviation stand for?

gal   (gallon)

in   (inch)

Jan   (January)

The items on this page to be shown to the students are typed

IN   LARGE   TYPE in the <u>Materials Book</u> for

use with an overhead or opaque projector.

13. ADD A LETTER
In each row of three words below, you can add the same letter at the beginning to create three new words. What are they?

___eat, ___troll, ___weep	(s)
___lane, ___recede, ___our	(p)
___hick, ___ill, ___read	(t)

14. NUMBER WORDS
The following definitions have to do with numbers. What are they?

two people singing together	(duet)
five children born together	(quintuplets)
seven days	(week)

15. SIMILES
A simile is a comparison of the two things using <u>like</u> or <u>as</u>. Complete the following similes with the names of animals.

stubborn as a _____	(mule)
sly as a _____	(fox)
poor as a church _____	(mouse)

16. EXPRESSIONS - ANIMALS
There are many names of animals in various expressions which we use frequently. Fill in the following blanks with names of animals.

_____sense	(horse)
_____Latin	(pig)
_____love	(puppy)

17. HOMONYMS
Homonyms are words which sound alike but are spelled differently. Spell a homonym for the following words.

our	(hour)
made	(maid)
new	(knew)

18. COMPOUND WORDS
A compound word is a combination of two different words. The first part of the following compound words is <u>black</u>. From the following definitions provide the complete word.

name of a fruit	(blackberry)
a reptile	(blacksnake)
a period of darkness	(blackout)

The items on this page to be shown to the students are typed

I N   L A R G E   T Y P E   in the <u>Materials Book</u> for

use with an overhead or opaque projector.

19. ANIMAL NOISES
Cows moo, but what noises do these other animals make?

turkeys	(gobble)
frogs	(croak)
doves	(coo)

20. COLORS
What color do we associate with the following things?

being cowardly	(yellow)
a revolutionary	(red)
in good health	(pink)

21. FAMOUS PAIRS
Many words occur in pairs. Complete each of the following pairs.

Mutt and _____	(Jeff)
Cain and _____	(Abel)
Jack and _____	(Jill)

22. EXPRESSIONS - ANIMALS
There are many names of animals in various expressions which we use frequently. Fill in the following blanks with names of animals.

That's a _____of a different color.	(horse)
A _____in hand is worth two in the bush.	(bird)
Don't count your _____before they've hatched.	(chickens)

23. HOMONYMS
Homonyms are words which sound alike but are spelled differently. Spell a homonym for the following words.

bear	(bare)
see	(sea)
week	(weak)

24. COMPOUND WORDS
A compound word is a combination of two different words. The first part of the following compound words is <u>red</u>. From the following definitions provide the complete word.

a bird	(redbreast, redwing, redbir
a British Revolutionary War soldier	(Redcoat)
a tree	(redbud, redwood)

The items on this page to be shown to the students are typed

I N   L A R G E   T Y P E in the <u>Materials Book</u> for

use with an overhead or opaque projector.

25. ANTONYMS
Antonyms are words that have opposite meanings. The following
words all have antonyms that rhyme with <u>rain</u>. What are they?

loss	(gain)
insane	(sane)
fancy	(plain)

26. GROUPS
A group of sheep is called a flock. What is a group of each of the
following called?

cows	(herd)
fish	(school)
bees	(swarm, hive)

27. AN EXTRA LETTER
Add one extra letter to the word on the left to come up with a new
word fitting the definition following.

cut - pretty	(cute)
din - to eat	(dine)
sun - submerged	(sunk)

28. NUMBER WORDS
The following definitions have to do with numbers. What are they?

a two-week period	(fortnight)
two thousand pounds	(ton)
ten years	(decade)

29. SIMILES
A simile is a comparison of two things using <u>like</u> or <u>as</u>. Complete
the following similes with the names of animals.

quiet as a _____	(mouse)
meek as a _____	(lamb)
bald as an _____	(eagle)

30. HOMONYMS
Homonyms are words which sound alike but are spelled differently.
Spell a homonym for the following words.

slay	(sleigh)
rose	(rows)
past	(passed)

The items on this page to be shown to the students are typed

I N   L A R G E   T Y P E   in the <u>Materials Book</u> for

use with an overhead or opaque projector.

86

31. ABBREVIATIONS
What do the following abbreviations stand for?

a. m.   (before noon, ante meridian)
R.F.D.   (Rural Free Delivery)
Tbsp.   (tablespoon)

32. NUMBER WORDS
The following definitions have to do with numbers. What are they?

eight notes on a scale   (octave)
four pecks   (bushel)
a hundred years   (century)

33. EXPRESSIONS - ANIMALS
There are many names of animals in various expressions which we use
frequently. Fill in the following blanks with names of animals.

_____in the grass   (snake)
to smell a _____   (rat)
buy a _____in a poke   (pig)

34. HOMONYMS
Homonyms are words which sound alike but are spelled differently.
Spell a homonym for the following words.

nun   (none)
hoes   (hose)
doe   (dough)

35. BOOK TITLES
The following are titles of children's books with the vowel letters
omitted. What are they?

Bmb   (Bambi)
Hd   (Heidi)
Sndr   (Sounder)

36. APOSTROPHES
If an apostrophe were placed in a particular place in the following
words, they would be different words altogether. What would they be?

shell   (she'll)
shed   (she'd)
were   (we're)

The items on this page to be shown to the students are typed

I N   L A R G E   T Y P E in the Materials Book for

use with an overhead or opaque projector.

37. **ANTONYMS**
Antonyms are words that have opposite meanings. The following words all have antonyms that rhyme with so. What are they?

fast	(slow)
yes	(no)
stop	(go)

38. **UP**
The word up is used in many expressions which we use daily. The following are definitions of expressions which include the word up. What are they?

to rob a store	(hold up)
to become happier	(cheer up)
picture of a pretty girl	(pin-up)

39. **FAMOUS PAIRS**
Many words occur in pairs. Complete each of the following pairs.

Amos and _____	(Andy)
Fine and _____	(Dandy)
Black and _____	(White)

40. **SIMILES**
A simile is a comparison of two things using like or as. Complete the following similes with the names of animals.

scarce as_____'s teeth	(hen's)
as funny as a barrel of _____	(monkeys)
slick as a greased _____	(pig)

41. **EXPRESSIONS - FOODS**
There are many names of food in various expressions which we use frequently. Fill in the blank with the name of something to eat.

Don't cry over spilt _____.	(milk)
One bad _____ will ruin the barrel.	(apple)
Don't put all your _____ in one basket.	(eggs)

42. **COMPOUND WORDS**
A compound word is a combination of two different words. The first part of the following compound word is house. From the following definition provide the complete word.

something to wear	(housecoat)
roof	(housetop)
a married woman in charge of a household	(housewife)

The items on this page to be shown to the students are typed

I N   L A R G E   T Y P E in the Materials Book for

use with an overhead or opaque projector.

43. WORD BLENDS
    A word blend is formed by combining parts of two words. Can you
    identify the two words from which each of the following words comes?

    brunch   (breakfast and lunch)
    smog   (smoke and fog)
    motel   (motor(ist) and hotel)

44. AN EXTRA LETTER
    Add one extra letter to the word on the left to come up with a new
    word fitting the definition following.

    cold - to fuss   (scold)
    seam - water vapor   (steam)
    own - a dress   (gown)

45. FAMOUS PAIRS
    Many words occur in pairs. Complete each of the following pairs.

    Romeo and _____   (Juliet)
    Punch and _____   (Judy)
    sugar and _____   (spice)

46. SIMILES
    A simile is a comparison of two things using like or as. Complete
    the following similes with names of food.

    thick as _____ _____   (pea soup)
    slow as _____   (molasses)
    bald as a peeled _____   (onion)

47. EXPRESSIONS - ANIMALS
    There are many names of animals in various expressions which we use
    frequently. Fill in the following blanks with the names of animals.

    Let sleeping _____ lie.   (dogs)
    It's raining _____ and _____.   (cats and dogs)
    The _____ can't change its spots.   (leopard)

48. -GRAPH-
    The root word -graph- meaning to write is part of many words which we
    frequently use. The following are definitions of words which contain
    the root -graph-. What are they?

    a picture   (photograph)
    an instrument for playing records   (phonograph)
    life's story written by the person himself (autobiography)

    The items on this page to be shown to the students are typed

    I N   L A R G E   T Y P E   in the Materials Book for

    use with an overhead or opaque projector.

89

49. ABBREVIATIONS
What do the following abbreviations stand for?

p.m.	(afternoon, post meridian)
Tsp.	(teaspoon)
in.	(inch)

50. ANTONYMS
Antonyms are words that have opposite meanings. The following words all have antonyms that rhyme with at. What are they?

dog	(cat)
skinny	(fat)
pointed	(flat)

51. NUMBER WORDS
The prefix tri- means three. The following are definitions of words which begin with tri-. What are they?

vehicle with three wheels	(tricycle)
three-fold	(triple, triplicate)
a stand with three legs	(tripod)

52. SIMILES
A simile is a comparision of two things using like or as. Complete the following similes with colors.

_____ as snow	(white)
_____ as indigo	(blue)
_____ as a gourd	(green)

53. EXPRESSIONS - PARTS OF THE BODY
Names of parts of the body occur frequently in various expressions. Fill in the blanks with names of parts of the body.

Keep your _____ peeled.	(eyes)
The cat's got his _____.	(tongue)
Keep your _____ to the grindstone.	(nose)

54. HOMONYMS
Homonyms are words which sound alike but are spelled differently. Spell a homonym for the following words.

heard	(herd)
tents	(tense, tints)
find	(fined)

The items on this page to be shown to the students are typed

IN   LARGE   TYPE   in the Materials Book for

use with an overhead or opaque projector.

55. PALINDROMES
A palindrome is a word that is spelled the same backwards and forwards.
The following are some definitions of palindromes. What are they?

sound of a horn or whistle	(toot)
the middle of the day	(noon)
female sheep	(ewe)

56. ADD A LETTER
In each set of three words below you can add the same letter at the
beginning to create three new words. What are they?

___are, ___ear, ___our	(H)
___luster, ___eel, ___ox	(F)
___ace, ___each, ___ark	(P or L)

57. FAMOUS PAIRS
Many words occur in pairs. Complete each of the following pairs.

stars and _____	(stripes)
horse and _____	(buggy)
law and _____	(order)

58. EXPRESSIONS - ANIMALS
There are many names of animals in various expressions which we use
frequently. Fill in the following blanks with the names of animals.

The early bird gets the _____.	(worm)
Take the _____ by the horns.	(bull)
It's the straw that broke the _____'s back.	(camel's)

59. HOMONYMS
Homonyms are words which sound alike but are spelled differently.
Spell a homonym for the following words.

piece	(peace)
rain	(reign, rein)
him	(hymn, hem)

60. COMPOUND WORDS
A compound word is a combination of two different words. The first
part of the following compound words is book. From the following
definitions provide the complete words.

one who reads a lot	(bookworm)
something to make books stand up	(bookend, bookshelf)
something to hold one's place in a book	(bookmark)

The items on this page to be shown to the students are typed

I N   L A R G E   T Y P E in the Materials Book for

use with an overhead or opaque projector.

61. SHORTENED WORDS
Many American words have undergone a shortening process. From what
longer words did we get these shorter words?

doc	(doctor)
gym	(gymnasium)
prof	(professor)

62. CROW
The word crow is used as a part of many expressions. What one word
or phrase containing crow fits the following definitions?

a bar of iron with a crook or claw	(crowbar)
in a straight line	(as the crow flies)
wrinkles around the outer corners of the eye	(crow's feet)

63. NUMBER WORDS
The prefix uni- means one. The following are definitions of words
which begin with uni-. What are they?

one part	(unit)
a mythical animal with one horn	(unicorn)
an outfit people like nurses wear	(uniform)

64. SIMILES
A simile is a comparison of two things using like or as. Complete
the following similes with the names of animals.

crooked as a _____'s hind leg	(dog's)
snug as a _____ in a rug	(bug)
as lazy as a _____ _____	(hound dog)

65. HOMONYMS
Homonyms are words which sound alike but are spelled differently.
Spell a homonym for the following words.

seen	(scene)
red	(read)
pail	(pale)

66. EXPRESSIONS - PARTS OF THE BODY
Names of parts of the body occur frequently in various expression.
Fill in the blanks with names of parts of the body.

The way to a man's _____ is through his _____.	(heart, stomach)
You put your _____ in your _____.	(foot, mouth)
Put your _____ to the plow.	(shoulder)

The items on this page to be shown to the students are typed

IN LARGE TYPE in the Materials Book for

use with an overhead or opaque projector.

92

67. ABBREVIATIONS
What do the following abbreviations stand for?

P.T.A.   (Parent-Teachers Association)
T.W.A.   (Trans World Airlines)
T.L.C.   (Tender loving care)

68. ANTONYMS
Antonyms are words that have opposite meanings. The following words
all have antonyms that rhyme with tin. What are they?

lose   (win)
out   (in)
fat   (thin)

69. NUMBER WORDS
The prefix bi- means two. The following are definitions of words
which begin with bi-. What are they?

a vehicle with two wheels   (bicycle)
glasses with two-part lens   (bifocals)
occurring every two months   (bimonthly)

70. EXPRESSIONS - ANIMALS
There are many names of animals in various expressions which we use
frequently. Fill in the following blanks with the names of animals.

See you later _____.   (alligator)
I'll be a _____'s uncle.   (monkey's)
You can lead a _____ to water but you can't (horse)
    make him drink.

71. HOMONYMS
Homonyms are words which sound alike but are spelled differently.
Spell a homonym for the following words.

grown   (groan)
hole   (whole)
wood   (would)

72. COMPOUND WORDS
A compound word is a combination of two different words. The first
part of the following compound words is black. From the following
definitions provide the complete word.

extortion by threats   (blackmail)
something to write on   (blackboard)
twenty-one card game   (blackjack)

The items on this page to be shown to the students are typed

I N   L A R G E   T Y P E   in the Materials Book for

use with an overhead or opaque projector.

73. UP
The word <u>up</u> is used in many expressions which we use daily. The following are definitions of expressions which include the word <u>up</u>. What are they?

confused	(mixed up)
to reverse direction	(back up)
to reach someone ahead of you	(catch up)

74. ANIMAL NOISES
Cows moo, but what noises do these other animals make?

hyenas	(laugh)
crows	(caw)
horses	(neigh, whinny)

75. FAMOUS PAIRS
Many words occur in pairs. Complete each of the following pairs.

Hansel and _____	(Gretel)
curds and _____	(whey)
tooth and _____	(nail)

76. SIMILES
A simile is a comparison of two things using <u>like</u> or <u>as</u>. Complete the following similes with names of food.

thick as _____	(molasses)
cold as _____	(kraut)
alike as two _____ in a pod	(peas)

77. EXPRESSIONS - PARTS OF THE BODY
Names of parts of the body occur frequently in various expressions. Fill in the blanks with names of parts of the body.

Don't lose your _____.	(head)
Put your money where your _____ is.	(mouth)
Sticks and stones may break my _____ but words will never hurt me.	(bones)

78. HOMONYMS
Homonyms are words which sound alike but are spelled differently. Spell a homonym for the following words.

holy	(wholly)
least	(leased)
fourth	(forth)

The items on this page to be shown to the students are typed

I N   L A R G E   T Y P E   in the <u>Materials Book</u> for

use with an overhead or opaque projector.

94

79. **FOREIGN NUMBERS**
The following are numbers under ten in a foreign language. What numbers are they?

dos (Spanish)	(two)
sechs (German)	(six)
quatre (French)	(four)

80. **MALE AND FEMALE**
What is the female counterpart of the following male terms?

lion	(lioness)
bull	(cow)
gander	(goose)

81. **COLORS**
What colors do we associate with the following things?

envy	(green)
purity	(white)
melancholy songs	(blue)

82. **NUMBER WORDS**
The prefix <u>uni-</u> means one. The following are definitions of words which begin with <u>uni-</u>. What are they?

a vehicle with one wheel	(unicycle)
one sided	(unilateral)
to join together as one	(unite)

83. **EXPRESSIONS - ANIMALS**
There are many names of animals in various expressions which we use frequently. Fill in the following blanks with names of animals.

Lord, love a _____	(duck)
it's a _____ 's life	(dog's)
drunk as a _____	(skunk)

84. **ACRONYMS**
Acronyms are words created by combining the initial letters or syllables of several words. What are the words from which the following acronyms were made?

Nabisco	(National Biscuit Company)
NASA	(National Aeronautics and Space Administration)
Radar	(Radio detection and ranging)

The items on this page to be shown to the students are typed

I N   L A R G E   T Y P E   in the <u>Materials Book</u> for

use with an overhead or opaque projector.

85. **APOSTROPHES**

If an apostrophe were placed in a particular place in the following words, they would be different words altogether. What would they be?

wed	(we'd)
ill	(I'll)
well	(we'll)

86. **JACK WORDS**

"Jack" is part of many words or expressions. Tell how "Jack" is associated with each of the following.

associated with diving	(jackknife)
used at Halloween	(Jack-o-lantern)
something we'd like to hit someday	(jackpot)

87. **BABIES**

Many young animals have special names. What is the young called for each of the following?

seal	(pup)
whale	(calf)
tiger	(cub)

88. **DOUBLE TALK**

Some of our English words and expressions are made up of two parts that are exactly alike, as <u>bonbon</u>. What are the double parts of those defined below?

father	(papa)
a prison in New York	(Sing-Sing)
a type of loose fitting dress	(mumu)

89. **HOMONYMS**

Homonyms are words which sound alike but are spelled differently. Spell a homonym for the following words.

claws	(clause)
coarse	(course)
mist	(missed)

90. **COMPOUND WORDS**

A compound word is a combination of two different words. The first part of the following compound words is <u>sun</u>. From the following definitions provide the complete words.

a browning of the skin	(suntan)
an instrument to show the time of day	(sundial)
inflammation of the skin caused by over-exposure to the sunlight.	(sunburn)

The items on this page to be shown to the students are typed

I N L A R G E T Y P E in the <u>Materials Book</u> for

use with an overhead or opaque projector.

91. **WORD BLENDS**
A word blend is formed by combining parts of two words. Can you identify the two words from which each of the following words comes?

splatter   (splash and spatter)
bookmobile   (book and automobile)
prissy   (prim and sissy)

92. **ABBREVIATIONS**
What do the following abbreviations stand for?

T.G.I.F.   (Thank God it's Friday)
U.S.N.   (United States Navy)
Ph. D.   (Doctor of Philosophy)

93. **FAMOUS PAIRS**
Many words occur in pairs. Complete each of the following pairs.

chapter and _____   (verse)
Anthony and _____   (Cleopatra)
Mason and _____   (Dixon)

94. **EXPRESSIONS - FOODS**
There are many names of foods in various expressions which we use frequently. Fill in the blanks with the name of something to eat.

It wouldn't cut hot _____   (butter)
It's like taking _____ from a baby.   (candy)
It's as easy as _____.   (pie)

95. **HOMONYMS**
Homonyms are words which sound alike but are spelled differently. Spell a homonym for the following words.

threw   (through)
throne   (thrown)
pain   (pane)

96. **NUMBER WORDS**
The prefix bi- means two. The following are definitions of words which begin with bi-. What are they?

Having two sides   (bilateral)
An animal with two feet   (biped)
person having two husbands or wives   (bigamist)

The items on this page to be shown to the students are typed

I N   L A R G E   T Y P E in the Materials Book for

use with an overhead or opaque projector.

97. AN EXTRA LETTER
Add one extra letter somewhere to the word on the left to come up
with a new word fitting the definition provided.

ten - a shelter made of canvas   (tent)
wad - a division of a hospital   (ward)
her - a man admired for his bravery   (hero)

98. SHORTENED WORDS
Many American words have undergone a shortening process. From what
longer words did we get these shorter words?

ad   (advertisement)
exam   (examination)
still   (distill)

99. PALINDROMES
A palindrome is a word that is spelled the same backwards and forwards.
The following are definitions of palindromes. What are they?

energy   (pep)
a title for a lady   (madam)
protective cloth worn under the chin   (bib)

100. GROUPS
A group of sheep is called a flock. What is a group of each of the
following called?

wolves   (pack)
kittens   (litter, kindle)
lions   (pride)

101. NUMBER WORDS
The prefix bi- means two. The following are definitions of words
which begin with bi-. What are they?

to cut into two equal parts   (bisect)
speaking two languages   (bilingual)
occurring every two weeks   (biweekly)

102. HOMONYMS
Homonyms are words which sound alike but are spelled differently.
Spell a homonym for the following words.

vein   (vain, vane)
wait   (weight)
one   (won)

The items on this page to be shown to the students are typed

I N   L A R G E   T Y P E   in the Materials Book for

use with an overhead or opaque projector.

103. ANAGRAMS
Anagrams are words made by rearranging the letters of other words.
Begin with the word on the left; rearrange its letters to arrive at
a new word which fits the definition provided.

live - wicked or bad   (evil, vile)
stop - a blot, a stain   (spot)
tame - a food   (meat)

104. -DUC(E)-
Many words can be formed by adding prefixes or suffixes to the root
word -duc(e)-. The following are definitions of three words. Can
you identify them?

to make smaller, lessen   (reduce)
person in charge of a train   (conductor)
one who finances a motion picture   (producer)

105. FOREIGN NUMBERS
The following are numbers under ten in a foreign language. What are
they?

uno (Spanish)   (one)
sept (French)   (seven)
tres (Spanish)   (three)

106. NUMBER WORDS
The prefix mono- means one. The following are definitions of words
which begin with mono-. What are they?

an eyeglass for one eye   (monocle)
one tone   (monotone)
exclusive control of one commodity   (monopoly)

107. HOMONYMS
Homonyms are words which sound alike but are spelled differently.
Spell a homonym for the following words.

flour   (flower)
presents   (presence)
ring   (wring)

108. COMPOUND WORDS
A compound word is a combination of two different words. The first
part of the following compound words is house. From the following
definition provide the complete word.

a barge used as a dwelling   (houseboat)
a party to celebrate taking possession of   (housewarming)
  a house
an insect   (housefly)

The items on this page to be shown to the students are typed

IN   LARGE   TYPE in the Materials Book for

use with an overhead or opaque projector.

109. **WORDS WITH THE SAME PARTS**
In each set of compound expressions below, half of the expression has been omitted. In each blank by the set will be the same word. Can you supply it?

_____stop, _____cut, _____cake	(short)
_____boat, _____fly, _____maid	(house)
horse_____, fire_____, dragon_____	(fly)

110. **-GRAPH-**
The root word -graph- meaning to write is part of many words which we frequently use. The following are definitions of words which contain the root -graph-. What are they?

the written story of someone's life	(biography)
a study of the earth, land, and sea	(geography)
a written signature by the person himself	(autograph)

111. **GOOD-BY**
The following are three words for good-by. From what language did they come?

adios	(Spanish)
au revoir	(French)
arrive derci	(Italian)

112. **NUMBER WORDS**
The prefix mono- means one. The following are definitions of words which begin with mono-. What are they?

one syllable	(monosyllable)
an oxide containing one atom of oxygen	(monoxide)
speech by one person	(monolog)

113. **EXPRESSIONS - ANIMALS**
There are many names of animals in various expressions which we use frequently. Fill in the following blanks with names of animals.

_____ court	(kangaroo)
to earn a _____ skin	(sheep)
to eat _____	(crow)

114. **HOMONYMS**
Homonyms are words which sound alike but are spelled differently. Spell a homonym for the following words.

patience	(patients)
principle	(principal)
morning	(mourning)

The items on this page to be shown to the students are typed

I N   L A R G E   T Y P E   in the Materials Book for

use with an overhead or opaque projector.

15. PHOBIAS

The meaning of the word <u>phobia</u> is fear of. What are people with the following phobias afraid of?

claustrophobia	(fear of closed places)
autophobia	(fear of being alone)
toxicophobia	(fear of poisons)

16. HOMOGRAPHS

Homographs are words that are alike in spelling but different in their meaning and pronunciation. The following provides the definitions of both meanings of homograph. Provide the word.

to conduct	a metal	(lead)
a movement of air	to twist	(wind)
to rip	a drop of water from the eye	(tear)

17. MALAPROPISMS

A malapropism is an incorrect word which sounds much like the correct word but has a different meaning. Identify the malapropism in the following sentences and tell what the proper word should be.

Mary was Joseph's exposed wife.	(exposed - espoused)
Please guard against cosmetic rays.	(cosmetic - cosmic)
Our principal is a very extinguished man.	(extinguished - distinguished)

18. WORD BLENDS

A word blend is formed by combining parts of two words. Can you identify the two words from which each of the following words comes?

electrocute	(electricity and execute)
chortle	(chuckle and snort)
travelogue	(travel and monologue)

19. EXPRESSIONS - PARTS OF THE BODY

Names of parts of the body occur frequently in various expressions. Fill in the blanks with names of parts of the body.

Two _____ are better than one.	(heads)
I have it on the tip of my _____.	(tongue)
Don't bite the _____ that feeds you.	(hand)

20. ETYMOLOGY

Words in our language have come to us from several other languages. From what language do you think we got each of the following sets of words?

soprano, madonna	(Italian)
camouflage, ballet	(French)
adobe, cigar	(Spanish)

The items on this page to be shown to the students are typed

I N   L A R G E   T Y P E   in the <u>Materials Book</u> for

use with an overhead or opaque projector.

EXPRESSIONALYSIS

ACTIVITY NO. 10

EXPRESSIONALYSIS

Purpose

The purpose of EXPRESSIONALYSIS is to examine or analyze the meanings of many colloquial, proverbial, or idiomatic expressions which students might encounter in their reading materials, and to provide an element of humor in this analysis as an aid in understanding these expressions.

Skills

Literal and figurative interpretation of expressions encountered in reading is the primary skill to be developed through this activity. All comprehension skills relating to unusual or unknown expressions may be developed. These comprehension skills may include contextual analysis, interpretation, and critical analysis of phrases or expressions.

Materials Needed

Miscellaneous art supplies may be needed for this activity.

Preparation and Instructional Procedure

1. Prior to student involvement in this activity, the teacher should discuss factors relating to language development, local dialect, regional expressions, and colloquialisms. This discussion should serve as a stimulus for an investigation into some of the expressions used in many reading materials.

2. A selection of unusual or confusing expressions which students have encountered should then be compiled by the students themselves. Although the teacher might begin by providing some illustrations, the majority of the expressions analyzed should be selected by the students involved.

3. For each expression selected, the following may be done:

   a. Have a student draw a picture illustrating the absurdity of the literal interpretation of the words used in the expression. Example: "He's all thumbs" may be drawn as a man with thumbs all over his body. Other illustrations are provided in the Materials Book and following this explanation.

   b. The student may then show this absurd and humorous drawing to the class and let them attempt to guess the expression he has illustrated.

   c. The figurative meaning of the expression may then be discussed by the entire class. Possible origins of that expression may be projected by the students, then related by the teacher, if known.

4. A list of all illustrations and expressions analyzed might be kept on file and added to periodically as others are encountered and discussed.

<u>Items Provided</u>

Pages 103-104 in this book and pages 76-77 in the <u>Materials Book</u> contain eight drawings which represent the literal interpretation of figurative expressions which we frequently use. These pages may be removed and duplicated for student exercises. Answers to these are as follows:

1. He's all ears.

2. She's two-faced.

3. He's a shady character.

4. His name is on the tip of my tongue.

5. The cat's got his tongue.

6. It's a pig in a poke.

7. It's the straw that broke the camel's back.

8. Don't choke the goose that laid the golden eggs.

After allowing the students to guess at what these may be, proceed by allowing them to draw their own.

To the student: In the blank space by each number write the expression which you think the picture is illustrating.

1. _____

2. _____

3. _____

4. _____

5._____

6._____

7._____

8._____

THREE ON A READING MATCH

Purpose

The purpose of THREE ON A READING MATCH is to provide a stimulating game to make reading a more interesting activity for the readers. In addition, prizes which are positively reinforcing to the participating students are awarded to winning teams or team members.

Skills

The specific skills of comprehension, word recognition, and vocabulary development may be developed through this activity.

Materials Needed

1. A THREE ON A READING MATCH board will be needed for this activity. A sample board reduced in size is shown at the end of this explanation. The squares in the center of this board may be library card pockets covered with colored adhesive paper.

2. Several small blank index cards will be needed. These cards are folded in half and 12 are placed in the colored pockets during each game. The folded card allows half to rest on the outside of the pocket for the students to view after that square has been chosen by a participant. Names of prizes are displayed on one half of one side of these cards.

3. Three sets of 2" x 3" cards may be prepared with the numbers 1, 2, 3, and 4 written on them for the participants to indicate their number responses. These may be stored in library card pockets, if desired.

4. Play money may be used if desired.

Preparation and Instructional Procedures

1. A selected story should be read by the students. (This game might also be based on a variety of reading materials or selections which the students have recently read or on specific skills in isolation. Samples of both follow this explanation.)

2. The selection of prizes is made. Although actual participation in the game itself in many cases is sufficient motivation, the selection of prizes is of extreme importance. All prizes should be items which are highly reinforcing to the participating students. This can be done first by selecting those items as prizes which the students indicate they would like to have. Observations of reinforcers should play a more major role in this selection. Although groups of students in different schools or areas would respond to various reinforcers in different ways, and although selection of prizes should be made on the basis of the characteristics of what is reinforcing to the specific groups involved, the following suggestions might be used as a starting point:

a. Money (usually one dollar)

b. Consumables
   (1) Edibles (candy, doughnuts, potato chips, etc.)
   (2) Drinkables (coke, punch, milk, etc.)

c. Tangibles or manipulatables
   (1) Toys (such as those found in dime stores)
   (2) Trinkets
   (3) Games or puzzles (small round inexpensive jigsaw puzzles, etc.)
   (4) Hobby items (stamps, pictures of baseball players, airplanes, etc.)

d. Free time (such as 10 extra minutes at recess, time for a favorite record to be played, etc.)

e. A grade of $\underline{A}$ for that reading lesson

An additional incentive would be for the groups to provide many of these reinforcers by doing such things as taking up 3-5¢ from each student for the $1.00 prize, having each team bring one prize, etc.

3. The THREE ON A READING MATCH board is then prepared by placing one folded 4" x 6" card in each pocket. On one half of these folded cards, the names of each of the four selected prizes are written three times, making a total of 12 cards. Each column contains four cards with a different prize written on each one. These are placed randomly behind the different colors. No one prize appears more than once in any one column. When the board needs to be changed, all cards in each column are taken out and quickly shifted to another position in that same column. This can easily be done without the participants' being able to see what is written on the cards, because the printed words may be hidden on the inside of the folded cards.

4. Several categories are selected from the reading material. Possibilities for the selection of these categories are limitless. They may be any topic relating to the reading selection itself or to the actual skills being measured. See Appendix for several examples of categories for all skill areas.

5. For each category chosen, four true-false questions should be prepared. Sample questions follow this explanation.

6. The entire class is divided into three teams. One member from each team is selected to begin. This team member may play the entire game for his team, or participants may change after every five-minute time period, after every fifth category has been selected, or some other predetermined procedure to allow for more student involvement. Everyone in the class will be "rooting" for his team member and the winning participant may share his winnings with his teammates (if possible or desired).

7. The three beginning participants sit at the front of the classroom in view of the THREE ON A READING MATCH board.

8. Three categories are shown to the participants. (Chalkboard may be used.)

9. Each participant selects the number of questions (from one to four) which he would like to answer if chosen. Prepared cards may be used to indicate the number desired, or the numbers may be written on a sheet of paper and held up by the student one at a time.

10. The amount of money for the "money pot" is then computed on the basis of the total number of questions selected by the three participants, multiplied by $10. For example, if the three selected the numbers 4, 3, and 4, the total for the "money pot" would be $110.

11. One participant is then selected to answer questions on the basis of the following:

    a. The participant who chooses the highest number of questions to answer is selected _if there is no tie for the highest number_. For example, if one participant selects _four_ questions to be answered, and the other two participants select _three_ or fewer, the one choosing _four_ will be allowed to answer the questions.

    b. If two participants tie for the highest number of questions, they are both omitted, and the remaining participant is selected to answer the questions. For example, if two participants have chosen to answer _three_ questions and the other participant has chosen to answer only _one_ or _two_, the first two are omitted and the latter will be the one selected to answer the questions.

    c. If all three participants select the _same_ number, allow them to reselect numbers.

12. The participant selected to answer the questions then chooses _one of the three categories and answers from that category the number of questions which he has chosen to answer_. Four questions are prepared for each category in case the number of four is chosen, but the participant choosing the numbers three, two, or one answers only three, two, or one question, respectively. He responds only with a "True" or "False" to that number of questions read to him.

13. When the selected participant _misses_ any of the selected number of questions, the total in the "money pot" is erased and a new round is begun.

14. When the selected participant responds correctly to all questions he is asked, he receives the entire amount of money from the "money pot". (Play money may be used if desired.)

15. After answering the selected number of questions correctly, the participant has the option of trying for a match on the THREE ON A READING MATCH board. Only upon answering correctly all of the selected number of questions is the option open for going to the board. If he passes this opportunity, he must wait until he wins another round before he has another choice of trying for a prize.

16. If the participant elects to try for a prize, he takes his accumulated earnings and views the THREE ON A READING MATCH board. This board contains columns of $20, $30, and $40 values with rows colored red, green, yellow, and blue. These twelve squares have four prizes hidden--each printed on cards behind three of the squares and each appearing only once in each column. For the participant to receive one of the prizes, he must uncover all three of the squares naming that prize which are hidden somewhere on the board. He does so by "buying" squares with the money he has accumulated, but he can "buy" only three squares in any one column, and he is limited to the amount of money he has accumulated to buy the squares. With $140, for example, he could uncover one of the $40 squares, two of the $30 squares, and two of the $20 squares, but no more.

17. If no match is made by a participant who elected to try for a prize, the others keep their accumulated money, steps 8-16 are repeated, and the positions of the prizes on the board change.

18. If a participant does uncover three identical squares for a prize, he receives this prize and may share it with his team members. Another round is begun if desired.

Origin of the Activity

THREE ON A READING MATCH was based on the currently popular television program "Three on a Match." Procedures for this activity were adapted from this television program for educational use in the reading classroom.

Items Provided

The following items are provided in this book and/or in the accompanying Materials Book:

1. Page 110 in this book contains sample questions which may be used for THREE ON A READING MATCH without a specific reading selection. These questions may be used to build word recognition skills.

2. Page 111 in this book shows a sample THREE ON A READING MATCH board. Only the inside section of the board is necessary if the categories are written on the board.

3. Pages 112-115 in this book and pages 78-84 in the Materials Book contain a sample story which may be used to illustrate THREE ON A READING MATCH.

4. Pages 116-117 in this book contain questions which have been prepared for the selected story for use with THREE ON A READING MATCH.

SAMPLE QUESTIONS FOR THREE ON A READING MATCH

(For use without a specific reading selection)

Phonics

1. The word bake contains a long a sound.	True
2. The word hike contains a silent e.	True
3. The word halo has two long vowel sounds.	True
4. The word church has five different sounds.	False

Antonyms

1. The antonym of humid is moist.	False
2. The antonym of reject is accept.	True
3. The antonym of daughter is brother.	False
4. The antonym of synthesis is analysis.	True

Four-Letter Words

1. Dunce is a four-letter word.	False
2. An antonym for narrow is a four-letter word.	True
3. The word phonics has a syllable containing four letters.	True
4. There are four letters in the word rodeo.	False

Syllabication

1. The word prism has two syllables.	True
2. The word strengths has two syllables.	False
3. The word measurements has four syllables.	False
4. The word antidisestablishmentarianism has twelve syllables.	True

Synonyms

1. False is a synonym for true.	False
2. Annoy is a synonym for irritate.	True
3. Delay is a synonym for procrastinate.	True
4. Lie is a synonym for fabricate.	True

Rhyming Words

1. The word g-o rhymes with t-o.	False
2. The word d-o-u-g-h rhymes with r-o-w.	True
3. The word f-r-e-a-k rhymes with b-r-e-a-k.	False
4. Words which rhyme have the identical final vowel and following consonant sounds.	True

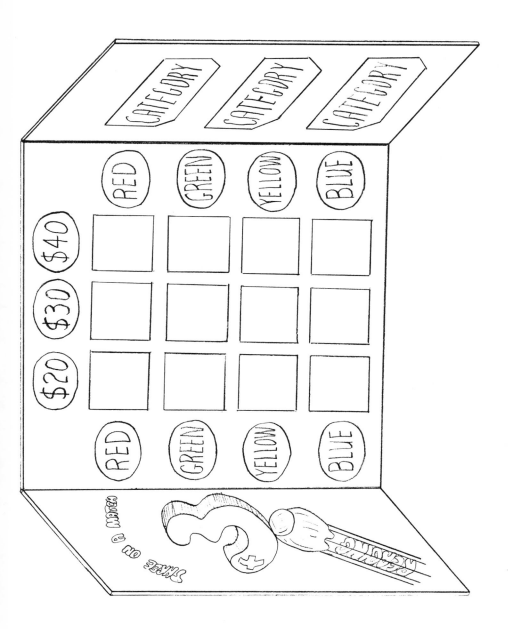

A SECOND CHANCE

by William R. Fowler

Flying your own airplane can be a very exciting thing. But it can also be very dangerous. Let me tell you a true story about how one of these exciting flights almost became my last.

On the day before Thanksgiving I left New Orleans Lakefront Airport at 7:02 a.m. The sky was clear and the morning sun was just peeping over the control tower as the plane lifted off the runway. With only one person aboard, my Tripacer (a small four-seat plane built by Piper Corporation) climbed quickly in the cool air. My plans were to fly to Jackson, Mississippi, attend a meeting that day in Jackson, then fly to Knoxville, Tennessee, for Thanksgiving Day. Upon arriving at the Jackson airport, I realized that a **tailwind** had boosted my actual speed to almost 150 miles per hour. That is a full 25 miles per hour faster than the plane cruises in still air.

After the meeting, which lasted most of the day, I checked into a motel for a good night's rest before continuing my trip. I awoke the next morning to heavy rain and gusty winds. It was so bad that the airport was closed to travel. According to the flight information service, the weather would not improve until around 4:00 the next morning. What a way to spend Thanksgiving Day--alone in a motel room! I decided that even though it would be dark, I would leave around 4:30 in the morning. There wouldn't be a chance at that time in the morning to replace the small amount of fuel already burned, but I could always stop on the way to refuel.

I was on the ramp and ready to go by 4:20 a.m. The sky was clear and the stars were out. At last I could be on my way. I was a little worried about flying in the dark because I had never done that before. But it was only a couple of hours until dawn, and off I went.

My flight plan called for a refueling stop at Chattanooga, Tennessee. However, again because of an unexpected **tailwind**, my speed was much better than normal. I arrived over the Chattanooga airport while still at 13,500 feet. Since it took more than 20 minutes to climb to that altitude, I didn't want to lose all that time by landing at this airport. I quickly calculated the speed, the amount of fuel left, and the distance to Knoxville. I decided that I could safely make it.

I decided to fly over the Smoky Mountain range rather than up the valley These mountains are beautiful but unpredictable. I did not realize that the winds at 13,500 feet had suddenly switched direction. Instead of a 20-mile **tailwind**, I was now getting nearly a 30-mile headwind. This meant that my actual speed was reduced by almost 50 miles per hour.

In approximately 20 minutes the engine began sputtering. The fuel was completely gone from the left tank. I quickly switched the gas selector to the right tank. At that moment I realized that I was not moving as fast as I had originally expected. I knew that the right tank had enough fuel for about 20 minutes flying time.

Realizing that I wasn't going to make it all of the way to Knoxville, I frantically began to look on the aerial map for small landing fields.

There were none close enough to make it. I double checked my
navigational equipment to make sure I was on the shortest possible course
to Knoxville.

I looked down at the mountains for a place that I might possibly make
an emergency landing. There was none! The mountains were steep with huge
rocks on top, and the narrow valleys were covered with trees. If I tried
to land here, it would mean certain death. As I picked up the mike, a
heavy sinking feeling came to the pit of my stomach. Was this going
to be the day of my death? I dialed 121.5 on my radio with a badly shaking
hand. This frequency is only used by airports and pilots when there is an
emergency. This was indeed an emergency. With a cracking voice I began to
transmit.

"Knoxville Tower, this is Piper 3535 Zulu, do you read?"

There was no answer. I tried again in an almost shouting voice.

"Knoxville Tower, this is Piper 3535 Zulu--<u>Mayday</u>, <u>Mayday</u>!"

A calm but firm voice answered. "Piper 3535 Zulu, this is Knoxville
Tower, may we help?"

I quickly answered without following proper radio procedures.

"Yes, I am on a heading of 280° approximately 50 miles from the
airport, and the fuel will be gone in no more than five minutes."

"Understand the situation 3535 Zulu, hold down mike button for 10
seconds for radar identification so we can pinpoint your exact location."

I impatiently held down the button for 10 long seconds.

"We have your location 3535 Zulu. Is there anyplace you can make
an emergency landing?"

"Negative!" I shouted. At that moment I felt the plane shake.
Although the prop continued to turn from the forward thrust of the plane,
the engine had stopped running. I was completely out of gasoline. I
glanced at the vertical speed gauge. I was losing nearly 1800 feet per
minute. The mountains were coming closer and closer. Would I be able to
glide over the next ridge? If I did, what would be waiting on the other
side? The ground came closer and closer. The plane skimmed over the top
by no more than 30 feet. There in the valley on the other side was a small
pasture between two mountain peaks. Could I make it? I had to try. There
was nowhere else to go. The Knoxville Tower was trying to contact me,
but I was too busy to answer. After all, what could they do for me? I
had to ride this one out myself.

I pushed the wheel in and at the same time turned sharply to the
right. The plane's speed increased to nearly 180 miles per hour, and at the
same time was losing nearly 2500 feet per minute. The ground looked as
though it was going to hit me in the face. As I was spiraling down between
the mountains to the little field below, I planned the exact point where
I would straighten it up and force it on the ground. As small as the
pasture was, I knew that it would take the entire field to get stopped.
Therefore, I had to get it on the ground on one end of the field. I finally
decided that one more spiral around the field would be the last. Still in
a steep turn, I got as close to the trees as possible. With the right wing
tip only inches away from the ground and the wheels nearly touching the
trees, I straightened out the bank and pushed the wheel forward which
forced the plane onto the ground with a loud thump! I was still moving at
over a hundred miles per hour. At this speed on the rough ground, the plane
kept bouncing back in the air. I held the wheel forward and pulled the
handbrake as hard as I could. The cattle were scrambling to get out of

the way, as the mountain at the other end of the field came closer and closer
The plane bounced to a stop only a few feet from the end of the field.

The only sounds I could hear were the buzz of the radio and the
thumping of my heart. I sat dazed as I pondered in my mind what had just
happened. Had I really survived an almost impossible ordeal? Slowly I
turned off the master switch and the radio and climbed out of the mud-spotted
plane. I looked around for signs of life besides the startled Black Angus
cattle.

About that time an old model Chevrolet came bouncing across the field
and rolled up beside the grounded plane. A lady and her four children
stared intently first at the plane and then at me. Finally she spoke.

"Howdy! I knowed there was something wrong 'cause all the geese
came to the house."

"Hello," I replied in a still shaking voice.

"I don't figure you or the plane got hurt none," she observed while
walking around the plane.

"I don't think so." I said. "Do you have any gasoline?"

"Nope, none you would want to put in there."

"How about farm gasoline--the kind you use in your tractors?" I insisted

"Oh, yeah, we got that."

"Would you sell me some of it?"

"If you want it, but will that thing burn tractor gas?"

"I don't know, but we'll find out."

She took me across the field up a narrow dirt road to where the
gasoline was stored. She found an old rusty five-gallon oil can, and filled
it with the purple-colored gasoline. (Purple dye is put in all gasoline
not used on public roads. This indicates that there has been no tax paid
on it and that it cannot be legally used in automobiles.)

When we arrived back at the plane, the highway patrol helicopter was
waiting close by. He had monitored my distress call. The officer asked,
"What are you going to do with that tractor gasoline?"

"Fly the plane out of here," I replied.

"I don't know whether you should or not," he said slowly while
watching me stand on the end of my suitcase in order to pour the gasoline
into the left wing tank. "It looks real dangerous. I don't even see how
you landed it in such a small field--much less be able to take it off,"
he pleaded.

I replied sternly, "If I made it in, I can make it out."

I must have still been in shock from the experience, because if I had
carefully considered my plight, I am sure I could never have attempted it.

The highway patrol chopper pilot reluctantly inspected the field for
holes and rocks, while I tried to start the engine. Finally, with a snort
and a backfire the engine roared into action. It didn't run too smoothly
but it did run. The chopper climbed to about 500 feet and hovered over to
the northwest corner above some trees. I taxied down to the far end of the
field--getting as close to the mountain as possible. I held the brake
tightly with my right hand, and slowly pushed the throttle in to the firewall
The engine sputtered and began turning faster and faster. The whole plane
shook and vibrated. I bit my lip, released the brake, and held the wheel
about three-fourths of the way back. The plane jumped forward and began
building up speed. I kept pulling the wheel backwards in order to keep
the nosewheel from bouncing so much on the rough ground. The mountain on the

other side of the field was getting closer and closer. I knew that I would only have one chance to do it right. So I waited until the last possible moment to pull the wheel all of the way back. As I did, the plane jumped off the ground. I very quickly made a sharp right turn. The wing nearly scraped the ground as the plane began a slow spiral up. After about seven or eight spirals, I was again higher than the mountains which surrounded the tiny field. I pointed the plane toward the Knoxville airport. The chopper which was waiting and watching followed me. The engine missed and ran roughly, but made it to the airport.

After landing at Knoxville and taxiing up to the flight service station, I shut the faithful old bird down. I had the balance of the tractor gasoline drained from the left tank. There was less than one gallon left. That would have been no more than five minutes. I really had been lucky. After looking death squarely in the face, I realized I had been given a second chance.

SAMPLE QUESTIONS FOR THREE ON A READING MATCH

Story: "A Second Chance"

Places

1. The pilot began his trip from New Orleans Lakefront Airport.	True
2. The pilot's flight plan called for a refueling stop at Chattanooga, Tennessee.	True
3. The emergency landing was made at Knoxville.	False
4. The pilot's ultimate destination was the Smoky Mountains.	False

Weather

1. On the trip from New Orleans to Jackson, the pilot encountered a headwind of 150 miles an hour.	False
2. On Thanksgiving Day in Jackson, Mississippi, the weather was clear and calm.	False
3. On the day after Thanksgiving the weather was clear and calm.	True
4. The pilot encountered a headwind before he reached Knoxville.	True

Hodge-Podge

1. This is a true story.	True
2. The pilot spent the night in Jackson, Mississippi.	True
3. The airport in Jackson, Mississippi, was closed for travel on Thanksgiving Day.	True
4. The plane the pilot was flying would seat four people.	True

Emergency Landing

1. The pilot made his emergency landing in a cow pasture.	True
2. The cause for the fuel reduction was a switch in wind direction.	True
3. When the left tank ran out the right tank then contained only enough fuel for 5 minutes flying time.	False
4. The emergency frequency number is 3535.	False

Words

1. <u>Zulu</u> is a word which pilots use to mean emergency.	False
2. <u>Chopper</u> is another word for a helicopter.	True
3. The word <u>aerial</u> means "having to do with radios".	False
4. The word <u>Mayday</u> is used by pilots to mean that they are flying at a distance of above 10,000 feet.	False

Speed and Distances

1. The pilot was approximately 50 miles from the airport when he radioed the Knoxville Tower.	True
2. A headwind causes a plane to go faster.	False
3. Immediately after the engine stopped running, the plane was losing nearly 1800 feet per minute.	True
4. After the pilot increased the speed to 180 miles per hour, the plane began losing 2500 feet per minute.	True

118

Objects

1.	Purple dye is placed in gasoline which is not taxed.	True
2.	The lady used a milk carton in which to carry the gasoline.	False
3.	The pilot used an orange crate to stand on to pour the gasoline in the tank.	False
4.	The automobile the lady drove was an old Ford.	False

Feelings

1.	The pilot was worried about flying in the dark.	True
2.	The pilot was excited about how he spent his Thanksgiving Day.	False
3.	The officer in the highway patrol helicopter felt skeptical about the pilot's flying his plane out of the pasture.	True
4.	The pilot felt confident that he would make it.	True

Words

1.	The word bird was used in this story to mean airplane.	True
2.	Tripacer was the name for a control tower.	False
3.	The word Piper was used to signal distress.	False
4.	The word negative was used to communicate "no".	True

Conclusions

1.	This pilot will probably not get low on gasoline in the future.	True
2.	The officer in the highway patrol helicopter probably concluded that all young pilots are fools.	False
3.	The lady probably concluded that her pasture would be used for a landing field in the future.	False
4.	The pilot will likely practice a "safety first" rule in the future.	True

Note to Teacher: As each question is attempted, place a check mark beside it. After all categories have been chosen, return to the category "Hodge-Podge" and use the unattempted questions left in each category.

SOCK
(SEQUENCE OF CARTOONS KWIZ)

Purpose

The purpose of the SOCK Game is to further develop the students'
reading skills by capitalizing on their pre-established interests in
cartoons.

Skills

The primary reading skills to be developed are the reading comprehension
skills of sequence and interpretation. Speaking activities may be used
as a correlated skill.

Materials Needed

1. Cartoons from the daily newspaper should be collected.

2. For each cartoon strip four to five 2" x 3" cards and one library
    card pocket will be needed.

Preparation and Instructional Procedures

1. The instructional procedure involves allowing the student to arrange
    each frame of a cartoon strip in the order in which he thinks it
    appeared in print. Each frame (including title) is pasted on a
    separate card and the student arranges these cards in the proper
    sequence at his desk. He then turns each card over to view the
    numbers on the back. If the numbers are in proper numerical sequence,
    the student has arranged the frames in the same order as they appeared
    in print. If not, he continues to think through the sequence. It is
    suggested that this exercise be used for fun and discussion of
    reading skills rather than for grades. Also, sequences other than
    the one which appeared in print should not be called "incorrect"
    or "wrong" but could be discussed according to why that sequence
    could or could not be logical.

2. If the SOCK game is to be used in a reading interest center in
    order to stimulate an interest in reading activities, the set of
    prepared cartoon strips may be displayed in this interest center of
    the classroom and may be used independently of specific reading
    selections. Students may examine the cartoon strips during their
    free time and may either keep their own record of how many they
    have worked or use a student record form prepared by the teacher.

3. When the SOCK activity is used by the entire classroom, the following
    steps should be taken:

    a. Circulate pockets of cartoon strips among participating students.

b. Allow them to arrange cards in order on their desks. Upon completion of desired sequence each student may recirculate his cartoons among those around him.

c. As a speaking exercise, the student may explain the sequence of frames in the cartoon strips to others. This is a particularly good speaking/thinking exercise when no words appear in any frame.

4. To prepare cartoons the following steps should be taken:

a. Cut from the newspaper or printed material those daily cartoon strips which can logically be arranged in only one order.

b. Mount each frame of the cartoon strip on a separate card. Also write or paste the title on a separate card. This will usually total four or five cards for each cartoon strip.

c. On the back of each card, number in the proper sequence so the student may turn the cards over to use as a self-checking device after he has arranged them.

d. If several strips of the same title are used, it will be necessary to be able to identify those cards belonging to the same strip (in case some cards become mixed). This may be done by using the initials of the cartoon strip itself and numbering each strip. (Example: For the first strip of "Peanuts," write P-1 on the bottom of the back of each card in the first strip, P-2 on the bottom of the back of each card in the second strip, etc. See example on following page.)

e. Place all cards for one strip in an envelope of some type. Library card pockets are excellent for this purpose. On the outside of each envelope, write the same number system as identified in step 4. (See following sample.)

f. Arrange in numerical order.

Adaptation

For those students who receive little challenge from arranging one cartoon strip in order, mix several strips for more difficult sequencing exercises. For example, in "Peanuts" strip, use P-1, P-2, P-3, and P-4 series in jumbled order. The student then faces two organizational difficulties for a further challenge.

POPPER

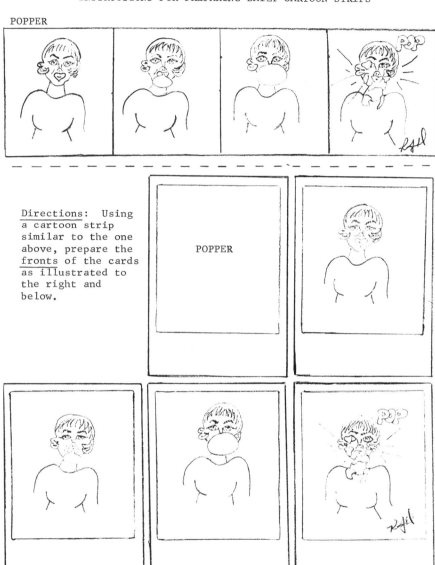

Directions: Using a cartoon strip similar to the one above, prepare the fronts of the cards as illustrated to the right and below.

POPPER

Prepare the <u>backs</u> of the cards similar to the following (½ actual size):

1	2	3	4	5
P-3	P-3	P-3	P-3	P-3

Prepare library card pockets to hold the above group of cards by writing the <u>number</u> of the cartoon series on the front as illustrated below (reduced in size):

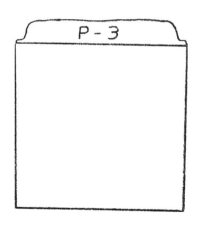

(Optional) Prepare a <u>box</u> to hold the cartoon series similar to the illustration below (reduced in size):

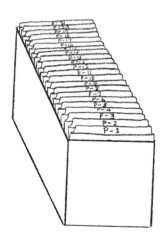

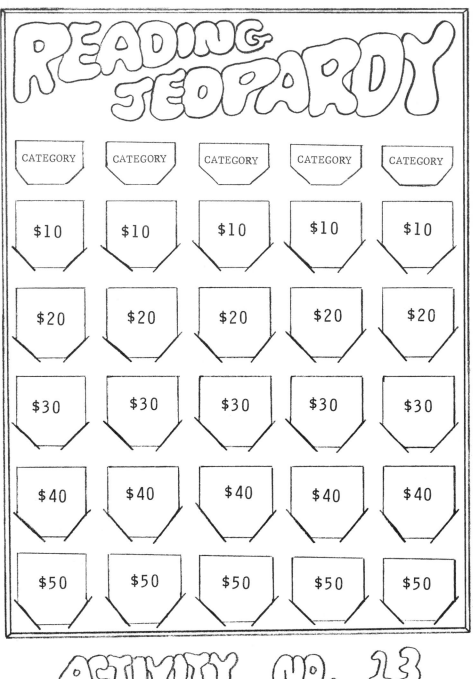

READING JEOPARDY

CATEGORY	CATEGORY	CATEGORY	CATEGORY	CATEGORY
$10	$10	$10	$10	$10
$20	$20	$20	$20	$20
$30	$30	$30	$30	$30
$40	$40	$40	$40	$40
$50	$50	$50	$50	$50

ACTIVITY NO. 13

Purpose

The purpose of READING JEOPARDY is to promote interest and enthusiasm in the development of the students' necessary reading and reading-related skills through a thought-provoking and competitive activity.

Skills

The specific skills of comprehension, word recognition, and vocabulary development may be developed through this activity.

Materials Needed

1. One READING JEOPARDY board is needed which may be made from a 22" x 28" sheet of oak tag poster paper with slots for categories and amounts. Several removable tabs (3½" x 1¼") for categories and 25 tabs (3½" x 3½") for amounts will be needed. A sample board (reduced in size) is shown on the cover of this explanation.

2. (Optional) A READING JEOPARDY transparency may be used with an overhead projector rather than a poster board. The form for making this transparency is provided in the Materials Book.

3. (Optional) Four "Cricket" Snappers may be used.

4. (Optional) Forms for preparation of READING JEOPARDY answers and questions may be used. These forms aid in organization when the students are preparing the answers and questions for the reading selection. They may also be filed for future use. A sample form is provided in the Materials Book.

Preparation and Instructional Procedures

1. A selected story should be read by the students.

2. Five categories of answers should be determined from this story. They may be any topic relating to the reading selection itself or to the actual skills being measured. Examples of categories which may be used may be found in the Appendix.

3. Five answer-question items of increasing difficulty must be prepared for each of the five selected categories. To do so, the answer to a question is written. Amounts (such as $10, $20, $30, $40, and $50 for Single Jeopardy and $20, $40, $60, $80, and $100 for Double Jeopardy) are determined for these answers according to the difficulty of each item. Either the teacher or the students may prepare these answer-question items.

4. While the students are reading the selected story, set the READING JEOPARDY board for either Single or Double Jeopardy.

5. The entire class is divided into 4 teams. Only one member from each team will participate at a time. Following every fifth question, team members may rotate. This allows 20 students to participate during each game. Money will accumulate for each team during the entire activity.

6. Select a student to start the game. He chooses the category and the amount.

7. Say, "The answer is . . . ." then read the corresponding answer to that category and amount selected.

8. When the answer is read, the student may respond by raising his hand. The teacher selects the student whose hand is first seen. If Cricket Snappers are used, the one heard first is selected to give the correct question.

9. If correct, the student receives the tab indicating the amount of money. Therefore, as the tabs are removed from the READING JEOPARDY board, the remaining categories and amounts may be seen. If the student is incorrect in his response, another participant may have an opportunity to respond. The student with the last correct question always indicates the new category and amount.

10. The winner at the end of the game is the student (or team) who has accumulated the highest amount of money.

11. After the students have become familiar with the game, daily doubles may be included. Write DAILY DOUBLE on a card and place behind one removable tab on the READING JEOPARDY board. Only the person who selects this item is given an opportunity to respond. Before his response he is allowed to wager all or part of his total, or up to $50 in Single Jeopardy and $100 in Double Jeopardy if those amounts have not been previously accumulated. If the response is correct, he adds this amount to his total; if incorrect, the wagered amount is deducted. (Incorrect responses may be ignored instead.)

12. If you choose to include a FINAL JEOPARDY question, this may be done without the use of the READING JEOPARDY board. Relate the category to the students, allow them to wager all or part of their total, give them the Final Jeopardy answer, and let each student write his answer on a sheet of paper. Reveal the correct response and have students add to or deduct from their totals.

Adaptations of Activity

The above rules may be altered to maintain interest or provide a variety of exercises in the following ways:

1. READING JEOPARDY could be played following the reading of several stories which may have been evaluated in other ways. The categories would be the story titles of those selections. For example, on Friday, after one reading selection has been read each day and other exercises have been used to determine reading progress following these lessons, the class may participate in a READING JEOPARDY game involving all five stories. Miscellaneous questions could be used.

2. READING JEOPARDY may be played to develop reading skills through the other content areas which the students are studying. For example, one game could be played to develop the vocabulary items or specific terminology in content areas such as mathematics, music, social studies, literature, etc. Or, each subject area could be divided into specific categories for vocabulary development, such as:

Mathematics: Terms used in Division, Multiplication, Algebra, etc.
Literature: Short stories, Novels, Poets, First Lines, etc.
Science: Biology, Chemistry, Scientists, etc.
Music: Instruments, Composers, Songs, etc.

3. The relationship of reading to the other language arts skills could be enhanced through the READING JEOPARDY game. The following are some examples: (a) A story could be read to a class as a listening exercise and the same READING JEOPARDY game could be played as if the students had read the story themselves. (b) The spelling of words found in one or more reading selections could be used for one game. (c) Dictionary drill could be used in a READING JEOPARDY game. One game suggestion would be to use the game as a preparation period for a reading selection with the following possible categories: Word Meaning, Pronunciation, Context, Spelling, Origin of Word, Parts of Speech, etc., of the words to be encountered in a reading activity.

Origin of Activity

READING JEOPARDY was based on the currently popular television program, "Jeopardy." Procedures for this activity were adapted from this television program for educational use in the reading classroom.

Items Provided

The following items are provided in this book and/or in the accompanying Materials Book:

1. Page 127 in this book and page 85 in the Materials Book provide a form which may be used to make a transparency for Single Jeopardy. A grease pencil may be used to write in the categories each time the game is played. Pennies may be placed on the transparency to show those which have been selected.

2. Page 128 in this book and page 86 in the Materials Book provide a form which may be used for Double Jeopardy.

3. Page 129 in this book and page 87 in the Materials Book provide a form which may be duplicated and given to students for writing their own answers and questions for READING JEOPARDY.

4. Page 130 in this book contains questions which may be used with READING JEOPARDY without the use of a specific reading selection.

READING JEOPARDY

$10	$10	$10	$10	$10
$20	$20	$20	$20	$20
$30	$30	$30	$30	$30
$40	$40	$40	$40	$40
$50	$50	$50	$50	$50

READING JEOPARDY

$20	$20	$20	$20	$20
$40	$40	$40	$40	$40
$60	$60	$60	$60	$60
$80	$80	$80	$80	$80
$100	$100	$100	$100	$100

FORM FOR PREPARING ANSWER-QUESTION ITEMS FOR JEOPARDY

Reading Selection: _____

Answers	Acceptable Questions
Category: _____	
$10 _____	
$20 _____	
$30 _____	
$40 _____	
$50 _____	
Category: _____	
$10 _____	
$20 _____	
$30 _____	
$40 _____	
$50 _____	
Category: _____	
$10 _____	
$20 _____	
$30 _____	
$40 _____	
$50 _____	

SAMPLES OF MISCELLANEOUS ANSWER-QUESTION ITEMS FOR READING JEOPARDY

(For use without a specific reading selection)

Answers	Acceptable questions
Category: <u>Words with long a sound</u>	
$10 - A body of water	What is a lake?
$20 - A particle of snow	What is a flake?
$30 - A synonym for tardy	What is late?
$40 - An antonym for work	What is play?
$50 - Something squirrels eat	What is acorns?
Category: <u>Young and Old</u>	
$10 - An adult female human	What is woman?
$20 - A young bear	What is a cub?
$30 - A young lion	What is a cub?
$40 - A young bull	What is a calf?
$50 - A young fox	What is a cub?
Category: <u>Rhyming Words</u>	
$10 - A word that rhymes with hat	What is (all rhyming words will be acceptable)?
$20 - A word that rhymes with toy	''
$30 - A word that rhymes with thing	''
$40 - A word that rhymes with school	''
$50 - A word that rhymes with father	''
Category: <u>Scrambled Words</u>*	
$10 - A word from unscrambled f-t-a	What is fat?
$20 - A word from unscrambled e-a-t-h	What is heat?
$30 - A word from unscrambled g-n-s-i	What is sing or sign?
$40 - A word from unscrambled d-o-r-w	What is word?
$50 - A word from unscrambled h-e-a-t-r	What is earth or heart?
Category: <u>Opposites</u>	
$10 - The opposite of begin	What is end?
$20 - The opposite of country	What is city?
$30 - The opposite of tardy	What is prompt, on time, etc.?
$40 - The opposite of sensible	What is ignorant?
$50 - The opposite of humid	What is arid or dry?

*To the teacher: These mixed arrangements of letters should be printed on large cards for easy visual rearrangement by the students.

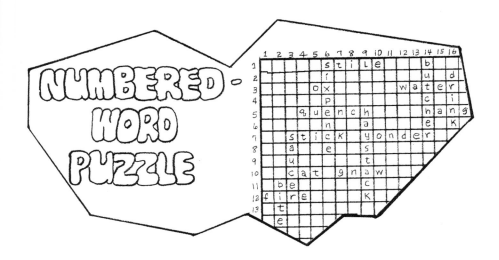

Story: "The Old Woman and Her Pig"

ACROSS

1-6   A set of steps for passing over a fence or wall

3-5   The animal the old woman wanted to drink the water

3-12 Liquid to quench the fire

5-4   Word meaning to put out or extinguish

5-14 What the woman wanted the rope to do to the butcher

7-3   Object which beat the dog

7-9   Word used in story to mean "at a distance"

10-3 Animal which began to kill the rat

10-7 Word which means to bite or chew upon

12-1 What the woman wanted to burn the stick

ACTIVITY NO. 14

DOWN

11-2 What the dog began to do to the pig

7-3   Object used to contain milk

1-6   What the woman used to pay for the pig

5-9   Where the woman found some hay

1-14 Person whom the woman wanted to kill the ox

2-16 What the woman wanted the ox to do with the water

Purpose

The purpose of the NUMBERED-WORD PUZZLE exercises is to allow the student both to work and construct word puzzles based on a reading selection. The forms available allow easy construction of the puzzles, eliminating such laborious problems as drawing lines or confusing the numbers. This exercise also provides an entire group the opportunity to work the same word puzzle.

Skills

The primary skill to be developed is that of vocabulary improvement. Word analysis and comprehension skills are also developed.

Materials Needed

1. Many duplicated forms for the numbered-word puzzle will be needed. A blank form is provided in the Materials Book.

2. Blank transparencies will be needed to make copies of puzzles to be projected when puzzles are to be worked by an entire group. This may be made from the blank form in the Materials Book.

3. (Optional) A "Puzzle Definition Sheet" may be used by the designer for each puzzle constructed. These forms may be filed for future use by the students. (See form in Materials Book.)

Preparation and Instructional Procedures

1. A selected story should be read by the students.

2. A puzzle must be constructed by the teacher or a student based on the content of this story. The following steps should be completed:

   a. On a blank duplicated form write in the words to be used in the puzzle.

   b. Number and define the words on the "Puzzle Definition Sheet" according to the illustration on the cover of this activity (reduced in size). Numbering for across and down responses consists of two numbers—the one found at the extreme left or right of the row, and the one found at the top or bottom of the column. The two numbers are separated with a hyphen. This numbering system is used no matter how many or how few words are used in each puzzle.

c. If students group themselves in pairs and construct puzzles for each other to work, two blank forms will be needed for each puzzle. One will be used by the student who constructs the puzzle for a record of correct responses and one will be used by the student who works the puzzle. On this sheet a red line may be penciled in by the designer at the bottom of each square that should be filled with a letter so that the student will be able to determine how many letters are in the word and what words cross each other; or, the student may use the number in the right hand column on the Puzzle Definition Sheet to determine the number of letters in the word. The student's original puzzle sheet may be used as an answer guide for the correct responses.

d. If one puzzle is to be worked by several students at the same time, it should be projected on a screen with an overhead projector. To do so, the words should be written in heavy pencil on the blank form. This sheet should then be sent through the Thermofax machine with a blank transparency film covering the puzzle. Numbers and word definitions may be copied from the Puzzle Definition Sheet onto the chalkboard. Before flashing the puzzle to be completed on the screen, each letter should be covered with strips of cardboard, pennies, buttons, beans, or some object which would cover just the squares to be used in that specific puzzle. Removal of these cover objects will reveal the correct responses.

3. Puzzles, Definition Sheets, and transparencies may be filed for future use.

Items Provided

The following items are provided in this book and in the accompanying Materials Book:

1. Page 134 in this book and page 88 in the Materials Book provide a blank NUMBERED-WORD PUZZLE form which may be duplicated.

2. Page 135 in this book and page 89 in the Materials Book provide a blank form which may be used on which to write the word clues for the puzzles.

NUMBERED-WORD PUZZLE

Story: _____

	1	2	3	4	5	6	7	8	9	10	11	12	13	14	15	16	17	
1																		1
2																		2
3																		3
4																		4
5																		5
6																		6
7																		7
8																		8
9																		9
10																		10
11																		11
12																		12
13																		13
14																		14
15																		15
16																		16
17																		17
18																		18
19																		19
20																		20
	1	2	3	4	5	6	7	8	9	10	11	12	13	14	15	16	17	

136

PUZZLE DEFINITION SHEET

Story: _____

ACROSS

Numbers (Row) - (Column)	Definition or Stimulus For Word	Letters in Word
_____ - _____	_____	_____
_____ - _____	_____	_____
_____ - _____	_____	_____
_____ - _____	_____	_____
_____ - _____	_____	_____
_____ - _____	_____	_____
_____ - _____	_____	_____
_____ - _____	_____	_____
_____ - _____	_____	_____
_____ - _____	_____	_____

DOWN

_____ - _____	_____	_____
_____ - _____	_____	_____
_____ - _____	_____	_____
_____ - _____	_____	_____
_____ - _____	_____	_____
_____ - _____	_____	_____
_____ - _____	_____	_____
_____ - _____	_____	_____
_____ - _____	_____	_____
_____ - _____	_____	_____

THE NEWLY-READ GAME

ACTIVITY NO. 15

THE NEWLY-READ GAME

Purpose

The purpose of the NEWLY-READ GAME is to provide a reading activity which would add an element of excitement to the evaluation procedure in reading--that of pairing male and female students and having them predict each other's responses to questions relating to the content of materials they have just read. Each participant should be stimulated to think seriously not only about materials he has recently read, but about the materials currently being read by his classmates.

Skills

Various aspects of comprehension may be developed through this exercise, particularly forming opinions, judging, evaluating, projecting, and appreciating.

Materials Needed

No special materials in the form of visual aids are necessary for this activity.

Preparation and Instructional Procedures

1. This game may be played centering around one specific reading selection, but it might be more effective if it centered around several reading selections which the students involved have recently read or around the books they are currently reading.

2. Questions involving opinion, judgment, evaluation, or appreciation should be formulated around these reading materials. Sample questions are provided at the end of this explanation.

3. Four couples are chosen to participate. Each couple should consist of one male and one female. (If the exercise would be more effective with the pairing of friends of the same sex, this change may be made.)

4. On the first round of the game, all the boys leave the room while the girls respond to a set of questions. The responses given by each girl should be those which she thinks will be the answer given by her partner when he returns to the room and is asked the same question. These responses are written on sheets of paper and saved. (One student in the listening audience could be assigned to each participant to record the responses.)

5. After the answers are given by the girls, the boys return and are asked the same questions. These responses are given orally.

6. For each response given by the boys which is the same as those given by their partners, five points are awarded to that couple.

7. For the next round, the girls leave the room and the same procedure for responding occurs, except that 10 points are awarded to each couple for a matching response.

8. In addition to the two rounds of questions of 5 and 10 point values, one 25-point bonus question could be added at the end of the last round. (This question should be very carefully chosen and should probably be a multiple-choice item.)

9. The couple with the highest total at the end of these two rounds is the winner.

Suggested Teaching Sequence

Due to the complexity of developing questions and to the reading purposes of this activity, this game would not be played as frequently as many other activities in this program. The frequency of use of this game would depend upon the amount of reading done by those participating. One such activity each month might be sufficient to fulfill the purposes of the exercise.

Origin of the Activity

THE NEWLY-READ GAME was based on the currently popular television program "The Newly-Wed Game." Procedures for this activity were adapted from this television program for educational use in the reading classroom.

Items Provided

The following two pages contain questions which may be used in the NEWLY-READ GAME.

SAMPLE QUESTIONS FOR THE NEWLY-READ GAME

At the first part of each round of the NEWLY-READ GAME, the leader says to the participant: "Predict how your partner will respond to the following questions." When the partner returns to the game, he is asked to respond to the questions orally. Many of the items in the questions below (such as titles of books or stories, authors or magazines) might be reviewed before the students play this game. This review would serve as a reinforcement of much prior knowledge and a stimulus for others to read more widely. For each blank space below insert the name of a specific book, poem, short story, etc., which the students have read or are currently reading. The following should be only samples of questions which you might use. Both you and your students may think of others.

1. What is your favorite book? (Possible limitations: Favorite poem, short story, magazine, newspaper, section of the newspaper, comic strip character, etc.)

2. What book would you like to read next?

3. Who is your favorite author? (Possible limitations: Favorite English author, American author, female author, male author, twentieth-century author, etc.)

4. Of the stories we have read in class, which one did you like the best?

5. Who is your favorite character in the stories (or books) we have read? (Possible limitations: Favorite male character, female character, fictional character, biographical character, etc.)

6. What section of the newspaper do you always read first?

7. What animal stands out most in your mind from the reading you have done?

8. What place stands out most in your mind from the reading you have done?

9. Which did you enjoy reading more, "_____" or "_____".

10. How would you rather "_____" have ended?

11. Who was your favorite character in "_____".

12. How would you rate "_____"?
    a. very exciting
    b. fairly interesting
    c. good
    d. poor

13. What book would you like most to give as a gift to a friend?

14. How do you feel about being given class time to read novels?

15. What is the most unusual thing you have encountered in your reading?

16. Complete this statement: Reading is _____.

17. Name one word to describe the character _____ in "_____".

18. What do you think of the emotional stability of the character _____ in "_____".

19. What do you think would have been the outcome if _____ (if the hero had been killed, etc.)?

20. Would you rather have as a close friend the character _____ in "_____", or the character _____ in "_____"?

   (The above questions of necessity had to be general in nature. A wide variety of more specific questions could be written following the reading of selected materials.)

CARTOON IQ

ACTIVITY NO. 16

CARTOON IQ
(Cartoon Inference Quotient)

Purpose

The purpose of the CARTOON IQ exercise is to further develop the students'
reading skills by capitalizing on their pre-established interests in
cartoons.

Skills

The primary reading skills to be developed are the reading/thinking
skills of inference and interpretation.

Materials Needed

1. Single-frame cartoons with captions (such as "Dennis the Menace")
   should be cut out of the daily newspaper.

2. One blank, unlined 5" x 8" index card will be needed for each cartoon.

Preparation and Instructional Procedures

1. From the daily newspaper choose a single-frame cartoon with a
   caption which will lend itself to interpretation through the
   picture. Not all cartoons can be used, for many captions contain
   humor in the actual words themselves without necessarily having
   a difference in expressions or situations depicted in the picture
   itself.

2. Trim the cartoon, clipping the caption. Leave only the title with
   the picture. Paste on a piece of stiff paper which is approximately
   one inch wider and four inches longer than the trimmed picture.
   (Blank 5" x 8" index cards may be used for most cartoons.)

3. Under the cartoon in a multiple-choice form, type the caption
   which actually appeared in print in a mixed arrangement with others
   made up to serve as distractors.

4. Number each card on the front (top).

5. Write the correct answer on the back of the card. This serves as a
   self-checking device and allows the materials to be self-instructional.
   (See the following page as an example.)

WELDON

No. 17

A. Are you gonna vote for George Wallace?

B. Did I tell you bout me 'n Geraldine?

C. Is you seven, or is you nine?

D. You know you's different from me? You's left-handed !

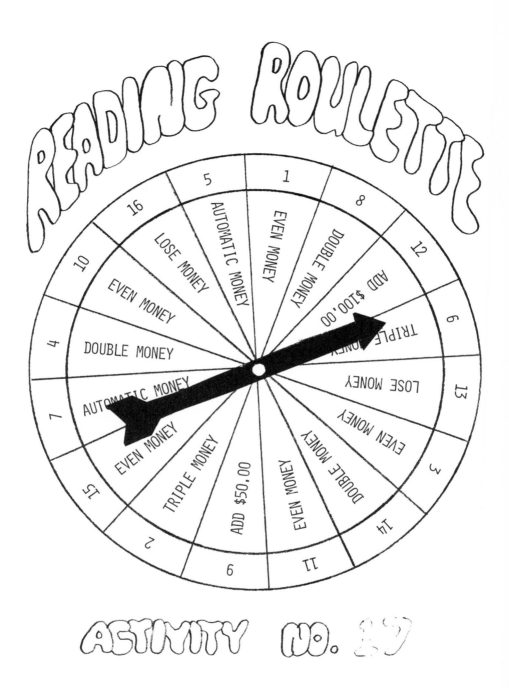

READING ROULETTE

Purpose

The voice of many disinterested male readers might echo, "Reading is dull! I hate reading!" The purpose of READING ROULETTE is to provide an activity for these students who find educational experiences dull. (Caution: Although all consequences result from setting the discs and twirling the pointer, and although no "gambling" is involved in this activity, the idea behind READING ROULETTE might be offensive to some individuals or families of those individuals. The teacher should determine this before introducing the activity.)

Skills

Literal and inferential comprehension skills may be developed through this activity. (A basic knowledge of multiplication and addition will be needed to compute individual scores.)

Materials Needed

1. One READING ROULETTE "Wheel" will be needed for every 2-4 students for this activity. This wheel consists of an inside disc, and outside disc, and a pointer which can be twirled. A sample wheel is shown on the cover of this explanation. Sample inside and outside discs are shown at the end of the explanation.

2. Play money may be used if desired.

Preparation and Instructional Procedures

1. A selected story should be read by the students.

2. Several questions should be prepared from this reading selection.

3. No more than two to four students should use one roulette wheel at a time. One of these students may be the "banker". If more students desire to participate at the same time, several roulette wheels should be made. Participating students should sit around the roulette wheel which is placed flat on a table or desk.

4. Students should decide how the inside and outside discs should be placed. These discs are independently moveable and consequences on the inside disc may be set to correspond with different numbers (from one to sixteen in mixed arrangement) found at the edge of the outside disc. On the inside disc are the following consequences:

   a. Even money: If the student answers the question correctly, he receives the number of dollars that he has twirled. If a student answers incorrectly, he neither receives nor gives up money.

b. Double money: If the student answers the question correctly, he receives double the number he twirled.

c. Triple money: If the student answers the question correctly, he receives triple the number he twirled.

d. Add $50.00: The student adds $50.00 to the number twirled if he answers the question correctly. The only student who receives $50.00 is the first to twirl this consequence.

e. Add $100.00: Same as (d), only $100.00 is added.

f. Automatic money: The student receives the number of dollars twirled whether or not he answers the question correctly. (He may receive an additional amount twirled by answering correctly.)

g. Lose money: The student must give up the number of dollars twirled. (He may gain it back if he answers correctly.)

5. The "banker" is given the responsibility of reading the question, checking for appropriate responses, and distributing the money. He chooses a person to begin the game.

6. The person chosen to begin twirls the pointer. He responds according to whatever consequence results.

7. The game continues until all questions have been used. At this point, the person with the most money is declared the winner.

Items Provided

The following items are provided in this book and/or in the accompanying Materials Book:

1. Page 147 in this book shows sample inside and outside discs which may be used as a READING ROULETTE board.

2. Page 148 in this book and pages 90-91 in the Materials Book contain a sample story which may be used with READING ROULETTE.

3. Pages 149-150 in this book contain questions which accompany the sample story for use with this game.

4. Page 92 in the Materials Book contains an instruction sheet which may be torn out and handed to the banker before the game is played. This sheet may be duplicated if more than one banker is used.

SAMPLE OUTSIDE DISC FOR READING ROULETTE

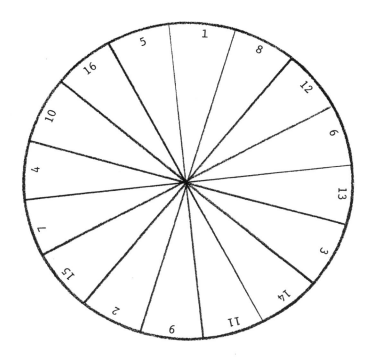

SAMPLE INSIDE DISC FOR READING ROULETTE

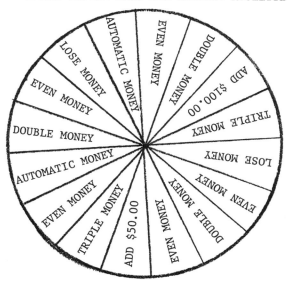

THE CRATER

by Charles Maynard

"A shell never hits the same place twice," thought John as he dived into a freshly made crater. He huddled in the bottom, hugging the ground, which was very warm from the explosion. Then again, as if to console himself, he said, "A shell never hits the same place twice." He winced and clutched his ears as a nearby explosion showered earth on him with a thunderous roar. Crouching a little lower, he again told himself, "A shell never hits the same place twice."

Suddenly, just as if someone had turned the war off, it was silent. John waited, straining to hear something, anything, just a sound, but it was silent.

Then, over to the left, he heard a painfilled cry which died to a moan. He cautiously peered over the edge of the crater, trying to see where the frightening horrid sounds were coming from. He saw a soldier and a medic running from crater to crater in search of the wounded man. Finally they stopped; they had found what they were looking for. John saw the soldier turn his head while the medic shook his. The soldier raised his pistol.

The shot cut through the air and the moaning ceased. Once again all was silent. John sank slowly back down into his crater and rolled over on his back. The sky was a dismal grey and his knapsack poked up into his spine. He started to remove it, but basic training told him not to. The fatigue was overbearing; he closed his eyes. The grey sky and lumpy knapsack melted away into numbness.

His mind began to wander. He thought of his coming furlough, which was just a week away. He thought of home and of the war. He remembered when the U. S. had entered the war. He recalled his enlistment and how proud his parents had been. He remembered how the church organ had blasted forth with "Onward Christian Soldiers" on the Sunday before he had left. He thought of Lynn, his girl, and the promises he had made to her. His mind wandered sleepily along the lane of his past and meandered up the path of his future. He thought of his triumphs and hopes, of his failures and fears, and of his darling Lynn. Her face was very vivid in his mind, even though two years and thousands of miles separated them.

His mind was drowsily wandering around, when, suddenly, a silent alarm deep from within, aroused him from his sleep. The sound of guns and explosions filled the air. He opened his eyes and the dismal grey sky had transformed into a menacing black. He quickly turned over and grasped his Springfield. He sensed that the Huns were about to attack. He readied his weapon. Then a thunderous roar filled his ears for a split second; then silence fell -- for eternity. A bigger crater had been formed at the spot where seconds earlier Johnny had been crouching . . . .

Seconds later a young soldier dived into the same crater saying confidently to himself, "A shell never hits the same place twice."

SAMPLE QUESTIONS FOR READING ROULETTE

Story: "The Crater"

1. What expression was used in this story by the two soldiers? ("A shell never hits the same place twice.")

2. What is a crater? (A hole made by an explosion)

3. How long had the crater been formed that John dived into? (It was a freshly made crater.)

4. It stated in the story "He winced and clutched his ears. . ." What does the word winced mean? (To shrink back, involuntarily)

5. In this story an explosion is heard, then a moan. What had happened to the soldier who was moaning? (He had been wounded.)

6. What was the final outcome for the soldier who was moaning? (He was shot.)

7. What was the role of the medic in this story? (He would have tried to save the wounded man if there had been hope.)

8. How did John feel physically? (Very tired)

9. What was John carrying on his back? (A knapsack)

10. What is a knapsack? (A bag strapped on the back used for carrying supplies.)

11. Why did John not remove his knapsack? (Basic training told him not to-- there might not be time to put it back on in case of emergencies.)

12. How did the color of the sky change during this story? (From grey to black)

13. "The fatigue was overbearing. . ." What does the word fatigue mean? (Tired)

14. What is a furlough? (A leave of absence from duty.)

15. How long was it to be before John could get a furlough? (One week)

16. "He recalled his enlistment and how proud his parents had been." What does enlistment mean? (The time when he joined the service.)

17. What was John's girlfriend's name? (Lynn)

18. What indication do we have that John and Lynn might have been serious? (He thought of her frequently and made many promises to her.)

19. How long had it been since John had seen Lynn? (2 years)

20. How far apart were John and Lynn? (Thousands of miles)

21. What song was played at church before John went into the service? ("Onward Christian Soldiers")

22. How did John's parents feel when he entered the war? (Proud)

23. "His mind wandered sleepily along the lane of his past and meandered up the path of his future." What does the word meandered mean? (To wander aimlessly or casually without urgent destination.)

24. "He thought of his triumphs and hopes. . ." What does the word triumphs mean? (A victory or conquest)

25. What kind of weapon did John have? (Springfield--rifle)

26. Who were the enemies? (Huns--Germans)

27. "Her face was very vivid in his mind. . ." What does the word vivid mean? (Producing a strong or clear impression on the senses)

28. ". . . and the dismal grey sky had transformed into a menacing black." What does the word menacing mean? (Threatening or dangerous)

29. Describe John's level of confidence about not getting killed when he dived into the crater. (He felt a shell wouldn't hit the place--but he was trying very hard to convince himself of that fact by repeating the statement over and over.)

30. What happened to John? (He was killed by another shell which hit the place he was hiding.)

31. What happened in the crater after John was killed? (Another soldier dived in saying the same thing John had said.)

32. Describe the level of confidence of the second soldier. (He seemed quite confident.)

READING HASH

ACTIVITY NO. 18

READING HASH
4 HOMONYMS
6 ANTONYMS
3 SYNONYMS
7 HOMOGRAPHS
SIMMER IN
THE MIND FOR
SEVERAL DAYS
TO DIGEST LATER
IN READING
MATERIALS

READING HASH
(Games with Homonyms, Antonyms, Synonyms, and Homographs)

Purpose

The purpose of READING HASH is to provide enjoyable, and competitive exercises to aid in developing four specific skills in reading. It is used independently of specific reading selections.

Skills

The reading vocabulary skills of building a knowledge of homonyms, antonyms, synonyms, and homographs may be developed through this exercise. In addition, some skills of structural analysis may be included.

Materials Needed

No special materials in the form of visual aids are necessary for this activity.

Preparation and Instructional Procedures

1. Prior to participating in each of the following activities the students should be encouraged to prepare their own lists of stimulus words for use with these activities. They should be allowed to use any notes or materials they have prepared only at the time during the game when it is their turn to present a stimulus word for which the opposing team must provide an appropriate response--no notes or lists should be used by the team attempting to do so.

2. All participating students should be divided into two opposing teams. These two teams line up and face each other at the beginning of each activity. One team is designated as Team A and the other as Team B.

3. Each of the following should be used as separate activities and might be played on different days if a combination would confuse the participating students. Each is explained as follows:

    a. Homonyms (For the purposes of this activity, a homonym will be defined as one of two or more words pronounced the same but spelled differently, such as to, too, and two. This is the technical definition of a homophone, but the term homonym is used instead because of its wider range of use in commercially published reading materials.)

        (1) At least one day prior to this activity the meaning of the term homonym should be fully explained to the students, with several examples given to them in written form. Before the day of the activity, each student (or teams of students) should think of several sets of homonyms which might be used in this activity. This makes a more personalized activity and causes greater interest and excitement than if previously prepared lists are given them by their teacher to learn.

155

(2) At the time of the activity the first member of Team A spells a word which has a homonym (such as r-a-i-n) to the first member of Team B. Within a predetermined time period (such as 30 seconds) the member of Team B must spell a homonym for that word (such as r-e-i-n, or r-e-i-g-n).

(3) If that member of Team B does not spell a homonym within the given time limits, he must be seated.

(4) If he does spell a homonym for the word given, he may remain standing. He then spells a word for which the next member of Team A must spell a homonym.

(5) This process continues until all members of one team have been seated. The team with remaining players is declared the winner.

b. Antonyms (An antonym may be defined as a word of opposite meaning.)

(1) At some time prior to this activity the meaning of the term antonym should be fully explained to the students, with several examples given to them in written form. Before the activity is played, each student (or team of students) should compile a list of several antonyms which might be used in this activity.

(2) When the game is begun the first member of Team A says a word which has an antonym (such as old). Within a predetermined time period the member on Team B must say an antonym for the word given (such as young or new). Through this activity, the use of negative prefixes, such as non- (nontoxic), in- (incomplete), dis- (disinterested), or un- (untie) should be encouraged.

(3) When the student fails to give an appropriate antonym, he must be seated.

(4) If he does give an appropriate antonym, he may remain standing. He then gives a word for which the next member on the opposing team must provide an antonym.

(5) This process continues until all members of one team have been seated. The remaining team is declared the winner.

c. Synonyms (A synonym may be defined as a word of similar meaning.) This activity is played identically to the antonym game with the use of similar meanings of words rather than opposite meanings of words.

d. Homographs (For the purposes of this activity, a homograph will be defined as one of two or more words spelled alike but having different pronunciations, such as read /rēd/ or /red/. This definition is not inclusive of many technical definitions which may be found; however, it will be sufficient for this exercise.)

(1) On the day prior to this activity the meaning of the term homograph should be fully explained to the students with several examples given to them in written form. Word parts homo- (meaning same) and -graph (meaning written) might be included in this explanation if it would be profitable to the class. Before the activity is played, each student (or team of students) should think of several pairs of homographs which might be used in this exercise. Homographs may be repeated within the same exercise.

(2) The activity is begun as the first member of Team A says a word which has a homograph (such as tear /tir/). The opposing member says its homograph (such as /taər/ within a given time limit.

(3) If the team member fails to respond correctly, he must be seated.

(4) If he does say an appropriate homograph, he may remain standing. He then gives a word for which the next member of the opposing team must say a homograph.

(5) The process continues until all members of one team have been seated. The remaining team is declared the winner.

Adaptations

This activity was designed to provide exercises in four problem areas of reading skills. However, the teacher may identify other problem areas which her class is experiencing with reading, and conduct a similar exercise to help solve that problem. These problem areas could be specific skills such as first sounds in words, middle vowels, consonant digraphs, etc. Students might respond with another word containing that same word element, or identify that element within the stimulus word given. Many such activities might be conducted in similar manner.

READING PASSWORD

WORDS

ACTIVITY NO. 19

READING PASSWORD

Purpose

The purpose of READING PASSWORD is to provide an enjoyable and competitive activity to develop the students' vocabulary relating to a reading selection.

Skills

The primary skill to be developed through READING PASSWORD is word meaning or vocabulary improvement. Word analysis and comprehension skills may also be developed.

Materials Needed

Several 2" x 3" cards might be used on which to write the stimulus words to be used in this activity. The chalkboard may be used to indicate score.

Preparation and Instructional Procedures

1. A selected story should be read by the students.

2. Words from this story which will be used as stimulus words should be selected by the teacher, nonparticipating students, or students who will be used as emcees for a participating group. Each word selected should be printed on two different cards (for simultaneous use with the two opposing teams).

3. One group of five students may play, and the remaining students may serve as a listening audience; or the entire class may be divided into groups of five so that all students may be active participants. These five will consist of two teams of two, and one emcee.

4. The duties of the emcee are as follows:

   a. Reveal the same word to one person on each team. Alternate showing the words to the members on each team.

   b. Keep up with the possible score for each round as follows: If the stimulus word is guessed on the first try by the team which begins, 10 points are awarded. If the member of the first team responds with a word other than the stimulus word, the second team attempts to guess the word. If **correct**, 9 points are awarded. This continues until a team member guesses the correct word, or until 10 attempts have been made to guess the word, unless the class decides to end the number of attempts at 5.

    c. Tally the scores for each team.

    d. Look up words that are questionable clues.

5. After the emcee shows a word to one member of each team, one team is selected to begin. The member who has been shown the word tries to get his partner to say the stimulus word by giving a one-word clue. No gestures or actions may be used to enact the word, though facial expressions may be permitted. These clues must be one word, must not be hyphenated, must not be part of the intended word, must not be spelled, and may be proper names. If the team member responds by giving one form of the correct stimulus word, one chance will be given to guess the correct form. If he doesn't guess it with this one chance, that word is thrown out, no one scores for that word, and a new word is given.

6. If the first team doesn't get the correct word, the next team is given an opportunity to try. This continues until one team scores or until the round is played out from lack of correct responses. The team member who is given the stimulus word always has the option to pass when it is his team's turn.

7. The game continues until one team scores 25 points.

8. Teams may change partners and play another 25-point game.

9. Each student may keep up with his individual score by adding his team's score for each game he plays. This reveals the individual's accumulated score, and a class winner may be declared, if desired.

Adaptation

1. Rather than using READING PASSWORD to follow a reading selection, it may be used to precede the reading of the selection as a readiness or preparation for that selection.

2. Rather than using READING PASSWORD to follow one reading selection, it may be used following several reading selections or following the reading of several books by the participating students. The stimulus words may be selected from titles or pertinent words from these reading materials.

3. If the entire class elects to participate in groups of five, the students may be grouped according to ability, with each group receiving a set of words whose level of difficulty corresponds with that group's ability level. This may also keep one group within the class from listening to words or word clues given by another group in another section of the classroom. Emcees selected for all groups, however, should be competent to fulfill their outlined duties.

Origin of Activity

READING PASSWORD was based on the currently popular television program "Password." Procedures for this activity were adapted from this television program for educational use in the reading classroom.

SAY THAT AGAIN

ACTIVITY NO. 20

SAY THAT AGAIN

Purpose

Many words are so overused in students' speaking and writing vocabularies
that problems arise when more difficult synonyms for these same words
are encountered in actual reading materials. The purpose of SAY THAT
AGAIN is to provide an exercise which allows the students to take an
overused word, such as "said" and explore synonyms for this word in
both their expressive and receptive vocabularies.

Skills

The comprehension skills of word meaning or vocabulary development, and
contextual analysis are enhanced through this exercise.

Materials Needed

No special materials in the form of visual aids are necessary for this
activity. Duplicated stories, however, should be provided for each
student.

Preparation and Instructional Procedures

1. A word which is extremely overused in the students' speaking and
    writing activities is selected as a target word. These words may
    be selected either by the teacher or students. Examples might be
    said, nice, great, happy, interesting, good, groovy, neat, etc.

2. Students should take a period of several days to think of all possible
    synonyms which they might use in place of the target word selected.
    A list should be kept of these words.

3. A reading selection which contains many of these synonyms should be
    typed, with blank spaces where the synonyms actually appeared.
    This selection may be chosen from the reading materials actually
    encountered by the students or may be written especially for this
    exercise. An example of the latter appears in the Materials Book.
    Each student should receive one copy of this story.

4. From the list of synonyms compiled by all class members, each student
    is to fill in the blanks according to which words he considers most
    appropriate for that specific context.

5. These versions may be shared with the other class members, if desired.
    Students should then be encouraged to use these synonyms in their
    expressive skills. Lists and exercises may be kept for future use
    and review.

A story entitled "Should They or Shouldn't They?" was written especially
to illustrate the exercise SAY THAT AGAIN (pages 93-94 in the Materials
Book and page 163 in this book). This specific selection gives the
students practice with using synonyms for the word "said". Following
a study of synonyms for "said", let the students compile a list of as
many synonyms as they can locate. This list may be similar to the one
on page 164 in this book. Be sure, however, to let the students compile
their own lists rather than provide one for them. Then duplicate the
story for each student to try to fill in the blanks with the most
appropriate synonym.

SHOULD THEY OR SHOULDN'T THEY

by Flora C. Fowler

Dusk was approaching the small town of Fairfield as the eight boys of the "RATHSCARE" quietly stole away from their homes for another secret meeting. They always met at the back of Sanders' garden, for there they could see the whole neighborhood, especially the Hardins' house, which was of particular interest to them this late summer evening.

"Okay, boys, we're all here," _____ Bobby, the club leader. "We've got to decide about the new boy who just moved in today. Do you think we should invite him to join our club?" he _____.

"We haven't even met him yet," Jerry _____. "Does anybody know anything at all about him?"

"His name's Randy." _____ Bill. "Randy Hardin. That's all I know."

"Wait, boys," Smally _____. "I think--"

"And he's twelve, like us," Bucky _____, "because I heard Mom tell Mrs. Hyder that all we needed was another twelve-year-old in the neighborhood."

"Do we have to decide tonight?" Walter _____. "If we wait until school starts, we'll know more about him."

Jim _____, "If we do wait, the 'SHARP CLAWS' will ask him to join their club."

"That's right," Jerry _____, "and nobody dares join both clubs."

"And besides," _____ Frank, "they have two more members than we do already."

"But," _____ Smally, "we can't--"

"I say let's invite Randy to join," _____ Tommy. "After we get his fifty cents entrance fee, we'll kick him out if we don't like him."

"I tell you," Smally _____, "Randy is--"

"Yes, we'll kick him out if we don't like him," Bucky _____, "like we should do to someone now."

They all turned and stared at Smally. Yesterday Smally had let them down by squealing to his parents about who had poured the molasses on old Mrs. Fritz's doorstep. Betraying one's "RATHSCARE" brother just wasn't done. Smally knew they would give him the treatment for awhile, and then things would be back to normal. So he would just remain silent for the rest of the evening.

Suddenly the back door at the Hardins' opened. Out stepped Randy. The boys peered through the hedge.

"Look, there he is," _____ Jerry.

"You're right," _____ Bill. "Let's see what he looks like."

"What funny-looking yellow shorts!" Walter _____.

"He must be from the city," Frank _____. "See how he walks."

"Why don't we go over and talk to him," _____ Bucky, "and if we don't like him, we won't ask him to join."

"Good idea," Bill _____.

"Let's go," Jim _____.

Seven boys raced to the Hardins' back yard. Only Smally remained in the garden. He knew Randy was a girl.

SAMPLE WORD LIST FOR SAY THAT AGAIN

For Reading Selection "Should They or Shouldn't They"

acknowledged	denied	iterated	requested
added	described	joined in	resounded
adduced	dictated	joked	restated
advocated	drummed	joshed	resumed
alleged	echoed	lied	retracted
announced	emphasized	lisped	returned to
answered	ended	maintained	reviewed
antagonized	enumerated	mentioned	sang
argued	exclaimed	mimicked	screamed
asked	explained	mispronounced	shouted
asserted	expressed	misquoted	sighed
averred	fibbed	mocked	speculated
began	giggled	murmured	spoke
begged	gloated	muttered	sounded out
believed	groaned	nagged	stammered
bellowed	growled	ordered	stated
bluffed	grumbled	persisted	stumbled
boasted	guessed	persuaded	stuttered
bragged	gulped	pleaded	suggested
called	hammered	pointed out	summarized
chirped	harped on	pronounced	surmized
claimed	imitated	protested	tantalized
coaxed	implied	prevaricated	tattled
commenced	indicated	questioned	taunted
commented	inferred	quizzed	teased
complained	informed	quoted	thought
complimented	inquired	read	told
concluded	inserted	recapitulated	tormented
contended	insinuated	recited	urged
continued	insisted	rehashed	voiced
decided	instructed	rehearsed	yelled
declared	interpreted	related	whimpered
defined	interrogated	reminded	whined
demanded	interrupted	repeated	whispered
demonstrated	intimidated	reported	

166

READING SQUARES

READING SQUARES

Purpose

The purpose of READING SQUARES is to develop the students' interest in reading by allowing them to participate in activities which they enjoy.

Skills

Literal and inferential comprehension skills may be developed through this activity.

Materials Needed

Four X cards and four O cards (each 11" x 11") are needed. The X and O cards should be of contrasting colors. Cards should be made from durable poster paper.

Preparation and Instructional Procedures

1. A selected story should be read by the students.

2. Several questions should be prepared from this reading selection.

3. Nine students are selected to sit in the following formation in front of the class: three students sit in three chairs placed side by side facing the class; three sit on the floor directly in front of the three seated; and three stand directly behind the three seated. (Formation is visually depicted on cover sheet of this activity.)

4. The remainder of the class is divided into two teams: Team X and Team O.

5. The first member of Team X selects a member of the "Reading Squares." The teacher asks this "Reading Square" a question concerning the reading selection.

6. The "Reading Square" may or may not know the answer. He has the choice of giving the correct answer to the question or "bluffing," but he must give an answer rather than respond with indecision.

7. The member of the team must then decide if he agrees or disagrees with the answer given by the "Reading Square."

8. If he agrees with a correct response, or if he disagrees with an incorrect response, he places his X on that square. This is done by letting that "Reading Square" hold the 11" x 11" card with a large X printed on it.

9. If he agrees with an incorrect response, or if he disagrees with a correct response, the O is placed in that square. (This is done unless it happens at a time during the game when placing the other team's symbol in the square would cause that opposing team to win. The team that wins must win by responding appropriately to the question for the winning square.)

10. The first member of the O team takes his turn in the same manner. This continues until one team wins the game.

Origin of the Activity

READING SQUARES was based on the currently popular television program "Hollywood Squares." The design of both activities was based on the popular pastime activity "Tic Tac Toe" or "X and O." Procedures for this activity were adapted from these ideas for educational use in the reading classroom.

Items Provided

The following items are provided in this book and/or in the accompanying Materials Book:

1. Pages 168-169 in this book and pages 95-97 in the Materials Book contain a sample story which may be used with this exercise.

2. Pages 170-171 in this book provide questions which may be used with the sample story.

3. Pages 98-99 in the Materials Book contain patterns for the X and O. These may be prepared as follows:

    a. Obtain two 22" x 28" sheets of poster board of contrasting colors. Cut each of these sheets into four 11" x 11" squares.

    b. Cut out of white or black 9" x 12" sheets of construction paper four X's and four O's.

    c. Paste these on the 11" x 11" squares of poster board.

    d. You are now ready to play READING SQUARES.

THE LAST MISSION

by Rickey Vance

Richard L. Ves was a sergeant in the United States Army. He was
considered by most officers to be the best demolitions man in the army
during the war with Germany.

Ves had about two more weeks before he ended a fifteen-year career in
the army. The war with Germany was about over and he had been on many
missions behind enemy lines. While planning his trip home, he received a
note from the captain telling him to come to headquarters. Ves had a
feeling he knew what the captain was going to ask him to do, but he went in
as if he had no idea why. His feelings were right. The captain had received
orders to destroy a plane being loaded with German bombs. Ves was chosen
to take what would be his last mission.

"Jump sight just ahead, sir," the pilot shouted. Ves had all of the
explosives and equipment he needed to do the job and was ready to jump at
the pilot's command. "Now!" shouted the pilot. Ves jumped out of the
plane that had taken him behind the enemy lines. He was soon on the ground
burying his parachute as he had done hundreds of times before. After he
had covered the jump equipment, he set out to find his target.

He had gone only about two miles when he began to notice he was going
to have a little difficulty getting to the plane. On the outskirts of the
camp there were many guards. Ves was armed with a gun, but with all the
Germans around, one shot would have them down on his neck in less than thirty
seconds. He was careful to pick out the best place to break through the
guards and get to the plane. He was tired from the two-mile hike and was
very worried about being in this much danger. Destroying half guarded
bridges and buildings was easy for a man of his talent, but he was never
in the middle of so many Germans in all the years of his career.

Crawling along on his stomach he was able to get past the guards and
within about twenty feet of the plane. There he had to cross a clearing
and plant the explosives under the plane. Checking to see that all the
guards were looking the other way, he made a break for the plane. He had
just reached the plane when a guard heard him running under the left wing.
The guard rushed over to see what had made the noise. Ves managed to swing
under the wing and pull himself up next to it. The guard stood by the plane
for what seemed to be a long time to Ves, but what was actually only a few
minutes. Holding himself up under the wing was very hard, for his fingers
were numb, sweat was dripping in his eyes, and he was getting so tired he
felt as though he would fall. He knew if he did he would be shot on sight.
As he felt his grip slipping, he saw the guard walk away.

He had lasted and had not given up his fight to stay hidden under the
wing of the plane. He had no time to congratulate himself, however. He
had to plant the explosives and set the timer before the guards came back
again. With the timer finally set, he looked to see if the Germans were
near. There were only two that he could see, and they were looking in the
other direction.

He made his break for the woods! He was almost out of sight when he

tripped. Hearing him, the guards opened fire. Ves returned fire on them
and started out for a nearby road where a car awaited him. The Germans
were close behind him and were getting closer by the second. They were
about to catch Ves only about a quarter of a mile from the car when the
timer on the explosives went off. The Germans were surprised by the
jolting explosion and hesitated for a few seconds trying to decide what to
do. Those few seconds were all Ves needed to get to the car. He drove
back to headquarters and announced that he had destroyed the plane.

He was given his discharge five days later and returned home to his
family. Even as an old man he would still like to tell the story of what
was almost truly his "last mission".

SAMPLE QUESTIONS FOR READING SQUARES

Story: "The Last Mission"

1.   What was the name of the sergeant in this story? (Richard L. Ves)

2.   With what country were we at war? (Germany)

3.   In what branch of service was Ves? (Army)

4.   How do we know Ves was experienced with demolitions? (The story stated that he was the best demolitions man in the army then.)

5.   How long did Ves have to go before he would be out of the army? (2 weeks)

6.   How long had he been in the army? (15 years)

7.   What did the captain order Ves to do? (Destroy a plane being loaded with German bombs)

8.   What did Ves do with his parachute? (He buried it)

9.   How do we know Ves was experienced with hiding parachutes? (The story stated he had done it hundreds of times before.)

10. Why did having a gun not make Ves feel very much safer? (One shot would have resulted in several Germans shooting back.)

11. Why was this job so different from what he was used to? (He was not used to the pressure of having so many Germans around.)

12. How did Ves hide from the guard at the plane? (He swung under the wing and pulled himself up next to it.)

13. How long did the guard stay near the wing of the plane while Ves was hiding? (Only a few seconds)

14. What was happening to Ves as the guard walked away from the plane? (His grip was beginning to slip.)

15. Which of the following words best describes Ves's mood as he was planting the explosives? (Curious, determined, cowardlike, conceited)

16. What kept the explosives from going off when Ves set them, thus blowing him up with the plane? (Ves used a timer to keep this from happening.)

17. What did Ves do to cause the guards to hear him? (He tripped.)

18. What did the guards do after they heard him? (They opened fire.)

19. How close was Ves to the car when the explosives went off? (¼ of a mile)

20. How did this affect the Germans who were chasing Ves? (It caused them to hesitate.)

21. How did this affect Ves? (It gave him time to get to his car.)

22. How long was it before Ves returned home? (5 days)

23. Why was this almost his last mission? (It was a close call.)

24. How did Ves feel regarding the mission? (Proud)

25. About how long did Ves live? (Until he was an old man)

READ-IN

Purpose

The purpose of the reading game READ-IN is to provide an enjoyable exercise for students to share their reading experiences. The game is played similarly to the television program "What's My Line?" except that panelists attempt to guess a character encountered in reading materials rather than the occupation of an individual.

Skills

Reading and reading-related skills may be developed through this exercise.

Materials Needed

READ-IN may be played without the use of added visual aids.

Preparation and Instructional Procedures

1. This activity is based upon a variety of reading materials such as specific reading selections or stories, books, magazines, cartoon characters, or newspaper figures.

2. A chosen student selects one character from all the material he and his classmates have recently read. This character may be real or fictional, man or animal, etc. During this activity the student will be asked questions designed to reveal his identity, and he must answer as if he were that character. He does not "act" like his selected character, but just responds to the oral questions. Careful selection of characters should be made. Students should be discouraged from selecting a character so insignificant that it would hardly be remembered by the other students. Teacher approval or approval from selected students might be considered.

3. A panel of four is selected to attempt to guess what character the student is presuming to be. Each panelist asks this student a question which can be answered with a "Yes" or a "No". Panelists ask one question at a time in order of their seating arrangement. Typical questions might be as follows:

   "Are you a comic strip character?"
   "Are you an animal?" (or human)
   "Are you male?" (or female)
   "Are you an adult?" (or child)
   "Were you a hero?" (or villain)
   "Were you in a book?" (or reading selection, magazine, etc.)

These questions would help to limit the possibilities so that more specific questions might be asked, such as:

"Were you a historical figure?" (Yes)
"Were you an American?" (Yes)
"Were you a president?" (Yes)
"Did you chop down a cherry tree?" (Yes)
"Are you George Washington?" (Yes)

or,

"Are you in the newspaper?" (Yes)
"Are you a cartoon strip character?" (No)
"Are you a columnist?" (Yes)
"Are you a female?" (Yes)
"Do you give advice?" (Yes)
"Do you have a twin sister?" (Yes)
"Are you Ann Landers?" (No)
"Are you Abby?" (Yes)

4. For each "No" response, the student is awarded 10 points. His object is to accumulate 100 points before the panelists guess his identity, but he must respond honestly at all times. The teacher should be told the selected character in order to help with answering when needed, or to guide in the questioning procedures when problems arise.

5. If the student does accumulate 100 points, the listening audience may then have an opportunity to **guess** his character. He is declared a winner for selecting a character which "outwitted" the panel of four.

6. The lower the score, the "smarter" the panel is considered to be when 100 points were not accumulated by the student.

Origin of Activity

READ-IN was based on the television program "What's My Line." Procedures for this activity were adapted from this television program for educational use in the reading classroom.

HEY, LOOK ME UP!

THE DICTIONARY

ACTIVITY NO. 23

HEY, LOOK ME UP!

Purpose

A skill which many students learn to avoid rather than learn how to use beneficially is the skill of using the dictionary. The purpose of HEY, LOOK ME UP! is to provide enjoyable and competitive exercises in reading-related dictionary skills. Learning information through this exercise may have more lasting effects for the students than simply being told this same information by their teachers.

Skills

The specific skills listed in item two under "Preparation and Instructional Procedures" may be developed through this activity.

Materials Needed

1. One dictionary will be needed for each participating student. These dictionaries should be alike for best results.

2. Large heavy paper will be needed on which to print stimulus words, phrases, or sentences for this exercise.

Preparation and Instructional Procedures

1. This activity may be used primarily in three different reading situations: (a) as a readiness exercise in preparation for the reading of a specific selection, (b) as a follow-up exercise relating to the words already encountered in a specific reading selection, and (c) as an independent exercise involving dictionary skills generally needed by average readers. Each is discussed separately as follows:

    a. As a preparation exercise:

        (1) A story should be selected for the students to read.

        (2) From the contents of this story a list of questions--the answers of which must be found in the dictionary--are prepared for class response. A list of sample questions follows this explanation. (This list does not relate to one specific exercise, but it illustrates such a possibility.)

        (3) Before this story is read by the students involved, the class is divided into two teams. These teams line up and face each other. (If class size is large, only a percentage of the team might participate at one time and alternate after every nth question.)

        (4) All students hold their dictionaries in hand as each question is read to them.

(5) As soon as the question is read to the two teams, each student then attempts to find the answer in his dictionary.

(6) The first student who finds the answer takes one step forward to indicate he has found a response. He does <u>not</u> give his response at this time.

(7) The remaining students continue in their attempts to locate the answer until a predetermined time period (such as 1 minute) has passed.

(8) At the end of this time period, the student who was first is asked to give his answer. If he is correct, he scores five points for his team. If he is incorrect, the first responding member of the opposing team is asked for an answer and is given five points if correct. All team members of both teams who stepped forward during the allotted time period will score one point for their team if they had located the correct answer.

(9) Team points are totaled following each question. Game continues until a predetermined score is reached by one team. That team is then declared the winner.

b. <u>As a follow-up exercise</u>: HEY, LOOK ME UP! may be played following the reading of a specific selection. The game is played similarly to the version described above except that the purpose is for the students to learn more about the selection they have just read rather than to prepare for reading it.

c. <u>As an independent exercise</u>: Any dictionary skill in which participating students may be deficient may be developed through a similar procedure. A variety of stimulus words or sentences are prepared centering around these deficient skills.

2. The following are some possible items for exploration with this exercise:

Word meanings
Alphabetization
Multiple meanings of words
(<u>or</u> Meanings of words in context)
Prefixes
Roots
Suffixes
Pronunciations
(<u>or</u> Diacritical respellings)
Accent(s)
Syllabication
Number of syllables
Word derivatives
Abbreviations

Verbal illustrations
Picture illustrations
Parts of speech
Word origins
(<u>or</u> Etymologies)
Proper spelling of words
Proper uses of words
Status labels (Obsolete, Archaic, Slang, Substandard, Nonstandard, Dialect, or Colloquial expressions)
Proper capitalization of words
Synonyms
Antonyms
Homonyms
Homographs

Any information which may be found in separate sections in the back or front of dictionaries may also be included as categories. Some examples might be:

Abbreviations	Rules of Punctuation or Spelling
Biographical Names	Symbols
Forms of Address	Vocabulary of Rhymes

ILLUSTRATIVE QUESTIONS FOR HEY, LOOK ME UP!

The following questions are designed to illustrate various types of questions which may be prepared for HEY, LOOK ME UP! In order to illustrate a wider variety of type of questions, these are not limited to the content of one specific reading selection. Questions are based on information found in Webster's Elementary Dictionary.

1. In this story someone drank from a demijohn. Describe what a demijohn looks like. (Hold up the following card.)

> ## demijohn

(Card is used for a question such as this in order to prevent the dual problem of both finding the answer to the question and also determining the spelling of the specific word to be looked up. It also aids in the visual memory of the word when later encountered in the reading selection.)

2. The following word is used in this reading selection. How many syllables does it contain? (Hold up the following card.)

> ## incorporeal

3. In this reading selection the following ancient city is mentioned. How is it pronounced? (Hold up the following card.)

> ## Byzantium

4. Our reading selection contains the following abbreviation. What does it stand for? (Hold up the following card.)

> ## C.

5. In this story a caddie carries Mr. Smith's golf clubs. How many ways can caddie be spelled correctly? (No card is shown.)

6. A city in Spain is mentioned in this reading selection. The following is a diacritical respelling of this city. How is it pronounced? (Hold up the following card.)

/ˈka-diz/

7. A sentence in this reading selection says, "No facsimile of this check may be produced." What does the word facsimile mean and how does it affect the check in this story. (Hold up the following card.)

facsimile

8. Our story mentions a dewlap on a cow. Where is the dewlap located on a cow? (Hold up the following card.)

dewlap

9. A dray is used in this story to carry a heavy load of wood. How many wheels does a dray have? (Hold up the following card.)

dray

10. The main character in this story plays a French horn. In writing French horn, which words, if any, would you capitalize? (No card is shown.)

11. The following word is used in this story. Does it rhyme with the word her? (Hold up the following card.)

shirr

12. In our story a sentence reads, "Mr. Conley retorted sharply." What is the prefix on the word retorted and what is the meaning of this prefix? (Hold up the following card.)

retorted

13. The mileage which Jerry got on his new car is discussed in this story. When adding the suffix -age to the base word mile, is the e on mile dropped? (No card is shown.)

14. The word spat has several meanings. In this story it is used as follows. What is the meaning of spat in this context? (Hold up the following card.)

> He wore a spat for decoration.

15. A disease called spavin is discussed in this story. Is this a disease you can get? (Hold up the following card.)

> spavin

16. The following word is used in this story as the name of a short-barreled lightweight cannon. On what syllable is this word accented? (Hold up the following card.)

> howitzer

17. The three-letter word fop is used in this story. Are you a fop? (Hold up the following card.)

> fop

18. In this story the hero was maimed. What happened to him? (Hold up the following card.)

> maimed

19. The colloquial expression shan't is used in the story you are going to read. What is shan't a contraction for? (Hold up the following card.)

> shan't

20. The word preserver is used in this selection. What is the prefix, the root, and the suffix in this word? (Hold up the following card.)

> preserver

HEAR YE!

ACTIVITY NO. 24

HEAR YE!

Purpose

Many older but less fluent readers need to engage in reading activities
which deal with sounds represented by letters or letter-combinations
within words. HEAR YE! provides an activity involving letter-sound
relationships which is not insulting to the older reader and can be
quite challenging. It can be used as a listening-reading activity
which dwells on both of these receptive language skills.

Skills

The specific skills of letter-sound relationships, spellings, sequence,
following directions, listening, and mental reorganization may be
developed through this exercise.

Materials Needed

No special materials in the form of visual aids are necessary for this
exercise with the exception of phases four and five. Sentence strips
or transparencies might be used for these two phases.

Preparation and Instructional Procedures

1. There are five phases of the activity HEAR YE! Each is described
   as follows:

   a. Phase one involves having the students listen to a sentence,
      then through mental reorganization combine the first letter of
      each word in that sentence in the sequence in which they were
      read in order to spell a word. Students should not be per-
      mitted to write as the sentence is read, but should wait until the
      entire sentence has been read before responding. Here is one
      example:

      She treated a cut knee. (Stack)

      This initial phase is to acquaint the student with this activity.
      (Additional lists of sentences are provided at the end of this
      explanation.)

   b. The second phase extends the same exercise, only each word which
      is formed will be a "command" word. Students are instructed not
      to write or call out this word, but to fulfill that command.
      Here is an example:

      Slowly trot around Nancy's desk. (Stand)

Notice that the sentence itself is a "command" sentence. Students who are not adept at following directions might confuse the actual sentence with the word to be identified. Such an exercise will help develop skills for these students. During this phase the slower students may avoid embarrassment by imitating the other students when one is encountered which they cannot think through. Therefore, this exercise could be used with an entire classroom of various levels of abilities without causing unnecessary frustration for the slower students.

c. Phase three of HEAR YE! uses the same skills of mental reorganization but the <u>last</u> letter of each word in the sentence is combined, in order, to spell a word. Again, the word spelled will be a "command" word, and the students are to perform this command. Here is an example:

Hit a small tack. (Talk)

At this phase difficulty is encountered for some readers. Thinking through these sentences will help build many important reading and listening skills. Perhaps having all students hold their response until a signal is given will allow more students to completely think through each sentence.

d. In phase four the student combines the <u>initial</u> <u>sound</u> of each word in the sentence. Again, the student is to carry out the instructions of the word, such as:

Cars run idly. (Cry)

At this point, the students might proceed from an exercise primarily involving the receptive skill of <u>listening</u> to the receptive skill of <u>reading</u>. The same sentences might be either visually portrayed on large sentence strips or projected on a screen with a transparency. The student <u>reads</u> rather than listens to a sentence and proceeds in the same fashion.

e. In phase five, the student combines the <u>final</u> <u>sound</u> of each word and proceeds in the same manner as above. An example is:

Cats like their tasty cream. (Scream)

2. For additional reinforcement, words other than "command" words might be used for phases three, four, and five.

3. Students should be encouraged to make up their own sentences to use with each other for any of these five phases. All sets of sentences could be kept on file for future use.

SAMPLE SENTENCES FOR PHASE ONE OF HEAR YE!

1.	Invite Sam.	is
2.	Always talk.	at
3.	Can a gnat eat?	cage
4.	Look at Carol eat.	lace
5.	Bandage a cut knee.	back
6.	Ride over a desert.	road
7.	Walk into the house.	with
8.	Find unlisted numbers.	fun
9.	Entertain all ranchers.	ear
10.	She treated a cut knee.	stack
11.	Cindy lost a small shoe.	class
12.	Knowledge is tremendous.	kit
13.	Could Larry or Cavin knit?	clock
14.	Never order raw, tough hamburgers.	north
15.	Roger eventually won a real diamond.	reward
16.	Everyone noticed John's only yearling.	enjoy
17.	Charlotte often finds fun easily enough.	coffee
18.	She'll call if everybody notices certain evidences.	science
19.	Rare engines are designed in Netherland gymnasiums.	reading
20.	Chad's houses are looking lovely, even near George's interesting new garage.	challenging

SAMPLE SENTENCES FOR PHASE TWO OF HEAR YE!

1.	You are weak now.	yawn
2.	Nobody owns Dodges.	nod
3.	Everyone always tries.	eat
4.	Will I need Kleenexes?	wink
5.	Mother offered a needle.	moan
6.	Sally's mother is like Emily.	smile
7.	Steven's kennel is priceless.	skip
8.	Send notices on return trips.	snort
9.	George received only a number.	groan
10.	Look over Victoria's equipment.	love
11.	Stop talking about new dresses.	stand
12.	Slowly trot around Nancy's desk.	stand
13.	Stop taking Orville's only plate.	stoop
14.	Will Richard involve the enemies?	write
15.	Sam tramped onto mother's plants.	stomp
16.	This harrassment is not knowledge.	think
17.	Louise is saving the eight novels.	listen
18.	Teddy once untangled Cherrie's hair.	touch
19.	George, I guess Gary likes everybody.	giggle
20.	These will interest several tourists.	twist
21.	Several quails united at Thomasville.	squat

SAMPLE SENTENCES FOR PHASE THREE OF HEAR YE!

1.	Whip a cat.	pat
2.	Oh, I hurt!	hit
3.	Is she slow?	sew
4.	Leave a part.	eat
5.	Crochet a map.	tap
6.	Roger, you turn.	run
7.	Hit a small tack.	talk
8.	Rob, I hurt Steve.	bite
9.	Jeb Rockwell, I can kick!	blink
10.	Pick ski resorts, Charles.	kiss

SAMPLE SENTENCES FOR PHASE FOUR OF HEAR YE!

(May be written on large sentence strips)

1.	Men only know.	moan
2.	Sonya is tired.	sit
3.	We eat peanuts.	weep
4.	He offers pennies.	hop
5.	Wilma ate vegetables.	wave
6.	Young elephants loaf.	yell
7.	Sue likes evil people	sleep
8.	We always like Kool-Aid.	walk
9.	Stores never open regularly.	snore
10.	Danny asked Nancy something.	dance

SAMPLE SENTENCES FOR PHASE FIVE OF YEAR YE!

(May be written on large sentence strips)

1.	Pick a lot.	cut
2.	Cheer a Nun.	run
3.	Whip Al today.	play
4.	Joel, we learn.	lean
5.	Ann, free Paul.	kneel
6.	Bailiff, I hurt!	fight
7.	Will Donna live?	love
8.	Look, Ma, Sheriff!	cough
9.	Cats like their tasty cream.	scream
10.	Scientists haul happy sheep.	sleep

THE READING ROADSTER

Purpose

The purpose of the READING ROADSTER is to use drivers' manuals to help teach the skills of word recognition and comprehension to remedial students who will not likely become fluent or superior readers. Older students classified as "non-readers" may through this activity learn some of the basic reading skills necessary to function as an independent adult.

Skills

The specific skills of word recognition and comprehension may be developed with remedial students. Several of these specific skills are discussed in detail in the explanation for this activity.

Materials Needed

1. A set of 40 miniature road signs may be prepared from two copies of drivers' manuals. Each sign presented in this manual may be cut out, backed with glue or double-stick tape, and mounted on 2" x 3" cards. A list of these signs is given in List 1 at the end of this explanation.

2. One or more additional drivers' manuals may be used.

3. Blank signs for various uses may also be prepared. Thirty-six blank white rectangular signs (2" x 1½") may be made from a 9" x 12" sheet of construction paper. Forty-eight yellow diamond-shaped signs (1½" x 1½") may be made from a 9" x 12" sheet of construction paper. The cutting line on these sheets may be drawn with magic markers and cut in the center of the thickness of the heavy mark. This gives a border for each blank miniature sign. Suggestions for mounting these signs are the same as given in Number 1. Possibilities for words for teachers or students to print on these blank signs for various activities appear in Lists 2 and 3 at the end of this explanation.

Preparation and Instructional Procedures

1. The road signs and drivers' manuals may be used to teach specific reading skills as follows:

   a. For Teaching Sight Vocabulary. The sets of signs may be used to develop a student's sight vocabulary. Many students with reading difficulties will recognize many of the 40 miniature signs because of their visual setting. The word "STOP" written on a red octagonal road sign, for example, might easily be recognized by students even though they may not recognize the letters S-T-O-P in other printed materials. Students should first be able to recognize the words on these miniature signs, then the same words could be written on separate cards. These cards could be typed with primary type, uppercase regular type, lowercase regular type, manuscript writing and cursive writing--each on a separate card. A matching exercise could then be formed with several different signs. This could proceed until the student had mastered this skill. Cards could then be limited to those with written words as stimuli for the development of a sight vocabulary. Fifty different words appear in the cards prepared from the drivers' manual. Words from Lists 2 and 3 may be used according to the student's individual needs. Additional words relating to driving skills may also be printed on cards for developing a sight vocabulary. These may come from the drivers' manual or from the student's own experiences.

b. For Teaching Phonics Skills. Signs may then be used to help teach some sound written-symbol relationships. Regular one-to-one correspondences may be taught first, then instruction may proceed to more difficult sound combinations or irregular spellings of sounds. An illustration of how a consonant blend might be taught might be the sp in SPEED LIMIT or the st in STOP. The vowel /ä/ or the conventionally named short o sound could be taught in such signs as STOP, DO NOT ENTER, or FALLEN ROCK. The lesson would extend from words encountered in these signs, to other words in the listening or reading vocabularies of the students, then to words which he does not already know. All phonics skills cannot be taught through these signs, but students may begin to form necessary generalizations concerning sounds with these words which are familiar to them.

c. For Teaching Structural Analysis. Some skills of structural analysis may be taught through the use of these signs. Words of more than one syllable may aid in teaching syllabication. Inflectional suffixes may be taught through the use of words in signs such as MERGING, FLASHING, TRACKS, PARKING, or PAVED. Derivational suffixes may be taught as they are encountered on signs noticed by the students. The concept of compound words may be taught through signs such as AIRPORT, PLAYGROUND, DRIVEWAY, or RAILROAD. Many skills dealing with word structure may be taught incidentally, either as the opportunity or need arises. An example would be the teaching of abbreviations when the sign LOW CLEARANCE 11 FT 6 IN is encountered.

2. Other Activities and Games

a. Sixteen of the signs prepared from the drivers' manual may be used to introduce a game similar to Concentration. These 16 (the first 16 on List 1) should be placed in rows of 4 face down on a table or desk in front of 2-6 students. One student would begin by turning over 2 cards. If these two cards contain identical words anywhere on the cards (such as LEFT TURN and RIGHT TURN both containing the word TURN), the student keeps those two cards and turns over two more. He continues until he turns over two which do not contain any words which are alike. These two cards are returned to their original face-down position, and the next student begins by turning over two cards and proceeding in like fashion. The game continues until all cards are used or until those which remain cannot be matched. The student holding the highest number of cards at the end of the game is declared winner.

b. Many similar activities may be formed from additional student-prepared cards. One suggestion might be to pair picture representations of information with words for that same picture.

Examples would be matching with RIGHT LANE ENDS, or

 with WINDING ROAD.

c. Students may be given blank cards to make a miniature sign for every actual sign they see within a set period of time. Some students will need help in writing or printing the signs they have seen. The object would be to observe, read, and write as many different signs as possible within this limited time period. Lists 2 and 3 offer many possibilities for these signs. Students may also be challenged to find as many signs as possible which do not already appear on Lists 1-3.

d. Students in groups may shuffle and deal selected cards for various purposes and activities. Two students may take 40 cards from the drivers' manual and draw one at a time from the single deck. As the student draws a card, he may keep this card if he is able to read this sign and/or give its meaning. When he is unable to do so, his opponent gets the card if he knows what the card says and means. Neither gets it if neither knows the desired information.

e. Students may be given a copy of a drivers' manual for a variety of other activities, ranging from skills of discrimination and matching like signs, to an eventual understanding of all printed material in the drivers' manual itself. It should be understood by the instructor, however, that all such manuals are not as "readable" as might be desired. Therefore, additional aid might be needed for comprehension difficulties encountered.

f. The students themselves may create many additional activities with the signs and manuals which will aid them in learning the necessary skills.

SIGNS FOUND IN DRIVERS' MANUALS

1. STOP
2. STOP AHEAD
3. YIELD (Yellow)*
4. YIELD (Red)*
5. DO NOT ENTER
6. DO NOT PASS
7. NO PASSING ZONE
8. NO PARKING HERE TO CORNER

9.

10.

11. LEFT TURN
12. RIGHT TURN
13. SPEED LIMIT 65
14. SPEED LIMIT 55
15. SPEED LIMIT 15 WHEN CHILDREN
        ARE PRESENT
16. SPEED LIMIT 15 WHEN FLASHING
17. RAILROAD CROSSING
18. FALLEN ROCK
19. SCHOOL
20. MERGING TRAFFIC
21. NARROW BRIDGE
22. CENTER LANE MUST TURN LEFT
23. EXIT 4 US 40 CHESTNUT STREET
24. 75 TENN
25. ONE WAY
26. KEEP RIGHT EXCEPT TO PASS
27. STOP OR SLOW
28. RR
29. 41 (Highway Number)*
30. (Children visually portrayed)*
31. (Red light)*
32. (Yellow light)*
33. (Green light)*
34. (Green arrow)*

35.

36.

37.

38.

39.

40.

SAMPLE CARD   (ACTUAL SIZE)

*Words enclosed in these parentheses are not actually printed on the signs but are portrayed visually.

WHITE SIGNS
(Indicating special law, regulation, or important information)

BUSINESS DISTRICT
BUS STOP
BUS STOP NO PARKING ANY TIME
CROSS AT PAVED CROSS-OVER ONLY
DEAD END
DEAD END ROAD
DEAD END STREET
DIVISION OF ROUTE AHEAD
DO NOT BLOCK ALLEY
DO NOT BLOCK DRIVEWAY
DO NOT BLOCK STREET
DO NOT PASS WHEN YELLOW LINE
  IS IN YOUR LANE
EMERGENCY STOPPING AND PARKING
  ONLY
END 15 MILE SPEED
END SCHOOL ZONE
5 MIN PARKING
5 MINUTE PARKING
FOOD AND FUEL NEXT RIGHT
JUNCTION OF ROUTES
KEEP LEFT
KEEP OFF MEDIAN
KEEP RIGHT
LEFT LANE MUST TURN LEFT
LEFT TURN ON GREEN ARROW ONLY
LITTER DEPOSIT
LITTER DEPOSIT AHEAD
LOADING AND UNLOADING ONLY
MERGE LEFT
MERGE LEFT INTO SINGLE LANE
MERGE RIGHT
MERGE RIGHT INTO SINGLE LANE
NO LEFT TURN
NO PARKING
NO PARKING ANY TIME
NO PARKING AT ANY TIME
NO PARKING BETWEEN SIGNS
NO PARKING IN THIS BLOCK
NO PARKING LOADING AND
  UNLOADING ZONE
NO PARKING LOADING ZONE
NO PARKING LOADING ZONE 8am-6pm
NO PARKING POLICE CARS ONLY
NO PARKING THIS BLOCK
NO PARKING THIS SIDE
NO PARKING THIS SIDE OF STREET

NO RIGHT TURN
NO STOPPING EXCEPT FOR REPAIRS
NO THRU STREET
NO TURNS
NO U TURN
1 HOUR PARKING
ONE WAY TRAFFIC AHEAD
PASS WITH CARE
PASS WITH CAUTION
RADAR CONTROL
RADAR CONTROL FOR YOUR PROTECTION
REDUCE SPEED AHEAD
RESUME NORMAL SPEED
RIGHT LANE ENDS
RIGHT LANE MUST TURN RIGHT
ROAD CLOSED
ROADSIDE BARREL
ROADSIDE TABLE
ROADSIDE TABLES
SCHOOL CROSSING
SINGLE LANE
SLOW SPEED BREAKERS AHEAD
SLOWER TRAFFIC KEEP RIGHT
SPEED LIMIT 45
SPEED LIMIT 55 TRUCKS 45
SPEED LIMIT 45 MINIMUM 30
SPEED ZONE AHEAD
STOP FOR SCHOOL BUS LOADING OR
  UNLOADING
10 MINUTE PARKING
THRU TRAFFIC USE LEFT LANE
THRU TRAFFIC USE RIGHT LANE
THRU TRUCK ROUTE
TRUCK ROUTE
TRUCKS KEEP 300 FT APART
TRUCKS USE LOW GEAR
TURN LEFT FROM LEFT LANE ONLY
TURN RIGHT FROM RIGHT LANE ONLY
TURN RIGHT ON RED WHEN CLEAR
$25.00 FINE FOR LITTERING HIGHWAY
TWO WAY TRAFFIC AHEAD
UNLAWFUL TO LITTER ON HIGHWAY
VISITOR INFORMATION
VISITOR PARKING
WEIGHT LIMIT 10 TONS
WRONG WAY

LIST 3

YELLOW SIGNS
(Warning of hazardous or unusual conditions ahead)

AIRPORT	LEFT LANE ENDS	ROAD NARROWS
BRIDGE OUT	LEFT LANE ENDS 1000 FT	ROUGH ROAD AHEAD
BUMP	LOW CLEARANCE	SCHOOL ENTRANCE
CATTLE CROSSING	LOW CLEARANCE 11 FT 6 IN	SCHOOL CROSSING
CHILDREN PLAYING	LOW SHOULDER	SCHOOL ZONE
CHURCH	MEN WORKING	SHARP CURVE AHEAD
CONSTRUCTION AHEAD	NARROW ROAD	SIGNAL AHEAD
CONSTRUCTION ENDS	PAVEMENT ENDS	SIGNALS AHEAD
DANGEROUS INTERSECTION	PAVEMENT NARROWS	SLIPPERY WHEN WET
DEER CROSSING	PEDESTRIANS	SLOW CHILDREN PLAYING
DETOUR	PEDESTRIAN CROSSING	SLOW CONGESTED AREA
DETOUR AHEAD	PLANT ENTRANCE	SLOW MEN WORKING
DIP	PLAYGROUND	SOFT SHOULDER
DIVIDED HIGHWAY	RIGHT LANE ENDS	TRAFFIC SIGNAL AHEAD
DIVIDED HIGHWAY ENDS	RIGHT LANE ENDS 1000 FT	TRAFFIC SIGNALS AHEAD
FIRE STATION	ROAD CONSTRUCTION	TRUCK CROSSING
FLAGMAN AHEAD	ROAD CONSTRUCTION 1500 FT	WATCH FOR ICE ON BRIDGE
HILL	ROAD CONSTRUCTION 1000 FT	WATCH FOR FALLEN ROCKS
HOSPITAL	ROAD CONSTRUCTION 500 FT	WATCH FOR SLIDES
JUNCTION	ROAD ENDS	

SAMPLE BLANK CARDS FOR MINIATURE ROAD SIGNS
(Actual Size)

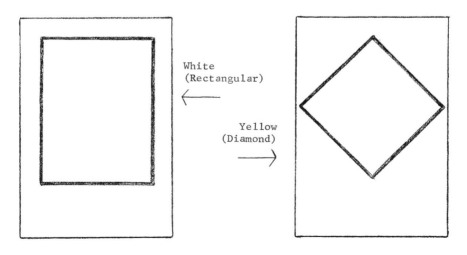

White
(Rectangular)
←

Yellow
(Diamond)
⟶

195

APPENDIX

SUGGESTIONS FOR CATEGORIES

Several games in this book require the use of the selection of categories and the writing of questions centered around those categories. The following pages provide some suggestions for categories which may be used for these activities.

Categories may be selected from items which will improve vocabulary, from the content of the story itself, from specific word recognition skills which the teacher is using in her classroom, from specific comprehension skills, or from miscellaneous topics.

Categories for Story Content

Abbreviations	Dates	Infatuation	Religion
Accidents	Days	Instruments	Rewards
Adventure	Directions	Joy	Romance
Affection	Doctors	Last Lines	School
Age	Drinks	Liquids	Science
Alphabet	Emotions	Love	Secrets
Animals	Excitement	Materials	Sights
Appearance	Exploration	Medals	Silliness
Attack(s)	Expressions	Medicine	Sins
Authors	Family Ties	Metals	Smells
Birds	Fantasy	Months	Solutions
Body Parts	Farm Items	Mother(s)	Sorrows
Books	Fashion	Music	Sounds
Brothers and Sisters	Fasteners	Musical Instruments	Sporting Events
Buildings	Father(s)	Mutiny	Stars
Business	Feelings	Mystery	Stimulants
Cars	Flowers	Names	Suspense
Caution	Food	Nicknames	Time
Characters	Fruit	Noises	Tools
Cities	Furniture	Numbers	Toys
Clothes (Clothing)	Games	Pain	Transportation
Colors	Garden Tools	Penalties	Travel
Communication	Ghosts	People	Trees
Conflict	Gobblins	Places	Trials
Conversation	Happiness	Plants	Truth
Correspondence	Heroes	Police	Vegetables
Countries	Heroines	Politics	Water
Cowboys	Household Items	Punishment	Weapons
Danger	Humor	Quotes	Weather

(Possibilities are endless and may be unique for each specific reading selection.)

Categories for Vocabulary Development

Four-letter words
Ten-letter words
  (Any number could be used)
Definitions (of words contained in the reading selection)
Phrases
Synonyms
Antonyms
Homonyms (Homophones or homographs)
Final Words
Famous Last Words
Prefixes ⎫
Roots ⎬ (Specific roots, prefixes, or suffixes
Suffixes ⎭ may be used as separate categories,
                such as -port-.)
(Etc.)

Categories for Word Recognition Skills

Rhyming words
One-syllable words
Two-syllable words
  (Any number could be used)
Number of syllables
First syllable of words
Second syllable of words
  (Any number could be used)
Beginning sounds (of specific words in story)
Middle sounds in words
Ending sounds in words
Words with long vowel sounds (mixed)
Words with short vowel sounds (mixed)
Words with /oi/ sound
  (Any sound could be used)
Consonant blends ⎫
Consonant digraphs ⎪ Careful use of terminology is suggested. Speci-
Vowel digraphs ⎬ fic examples for categories, such as "ai words"
Vowel diphthongs ⎭ or "bl words" might be a wiser category selection
                   than terminology which might confuse the student.
Pronunciation (Stimulus words in story are presented diacritically on
  large cards)
Sight vocabulary (Words which students should be able to recognize on
  sight are presented on large cards)
Words beginning with s-
Words beginning with th-
  (Any letter or letter combination might be used)
Fifth letter of words
Fourth letter of words
Last letter of words
  (Any letter could be used)
(Etc.)

Categories for Comprehension

Comprehension (1) - (Literal Comprehension Skills)
Comprehension (2) - (Inferential Comprehension Skills)
Details:

When	Who	}	Not suggested for
Why	What	}	the WHO, WHAT, OR
How Much	Where	}	WHERE READING GAME

Sequence (of events in the selection)
Main Ideas
Words in Context (On large cards, sentences are written with one word
                  underlined. Student must give meaning of underlined
                  word in that specific context.)
(Etc.)

Miscellaneous Categories (Any type of question)

Hodge-podge
Odds and Ends
Scrambled Words (letters in significant words are scrambled and presented
        on large cards to be unscrambled)
Surprise Questions
(Etc.)